Cameos in History and Culture 4

Ancient Roman Literature

Volume I: Poetry

Krishna Chaitanya

GW00496554

Sangam Books

SANGAM BOOKS LIMITED
57 London Fruit Exchange
Brushfield Street
London E1 6EP, U.K.

By arrangement with
Orient Longman Limited
3-6-272, Himayatnagar
Hyderabad 500 029 (A.P.), INDIA

© Orient Longman Limited 1966, 1997

Published by
SANGAM BOOKS LIMITED 1997

ISBN 0 86311 742 2

A catalogue record for this book is
available from the British Library

Typeset by
OSDATA
Hyderabad 500 029

Printed in offset at
NPT Offset Pvt. Ltd.
Chennai 600 014

To Biswanath

Publisher's Note

Between 1964 and 1966 Orient Longman Limited had published a series of four volumes by Krishna Chaitanya titled 'A History of World Literature'. The books have now been brought out under Orient Longman's new series *'Cameos in History and Culture'*.

In the third of the original volumes, the author had continued his work on the various aspects of ancient Roman literature. As part of the new *Cameo* series, the book has been reissued as two seperate volumes. The present volume, *Cameo 4*, deals with ancient Roman poetry while *Cameo 5*, deals with ancient Roman drama and literary thought.

These books present the quintessential beauty and wisdom of the world's literary legacies and are as significant today, as they were when first published.

The author, Krishna Chaitanya, was the recipient of the Padma Shri and other national honours. He passed away in June 1995.

Preface

This is the third volume in the series on the history of world literature. The earlier two volumes covered ancient Mesopotamia and Egypt.

As Latin was the language of ancient Rome, this work should perhaps have been called a history of Latin Literature. But Latin was the language not only of classical but also of pagan Rome. It continued to be the language of European Christendom as well, long after the Roman race had perished and the vast onrush of Germanic tribes had recast the ethnic map of Europe. Only a volume which covers the literature of both the periods can be justifiably called a history of Latin literature. The later phase, however, is not included in this volume. The reason is that the advent of Christianity brought about radical transformations in the temper of mind and heart, in the views about the world, man and man's destiny. Therefore, though the language continued to be the same, literature reflected a radically different culture mentality. This mentality had its origins in the profound experiences of the Jewish race. It confronted paganism in a long struggle and ultimately dominated it, although there were considerable unconscious assimilations as well. Therefore, we can resume our account of the history of Latin literature in the Christian era, only after we have studied the ancient literature of the Jews in a forthcoming volume.

The long stability of a theocratic system slowed the tempo of historic change in ancient Egypt. The clash of democracy, oligarchy, the dictatorship of the tyrants and the imperialistic ambitions of Macedonia accelerated the tempo in Greece. But it is in Rome that the tempo of historical change obtained such a heady acceleration that the tumult of those conflicts is astonishingly like the clamour of the conflicts of our own times. The seizure of power by the entrenched, landed aristocracy, the progressive deterioration of the middle classes, the increasing helplessness of the peasant in the rural areas and the worker in the urban, and the emergence of national consciousness in the various peoples governed by Rome made the conflicts bitter, protracted, extensive. Here, the history of Rome has great lessons for our own times.

Ancient India had contacts with Rome although they were not as close as those with Greece, being confined mostly to trade. It could be the case that the goddess in the temple of Cranganore (Kondungalloor) in Kerala was originally the deity of a temple erected for the worship of a Roman garrison stationed there to look after trade interests. But intimate cross-fertilisations in cultural traditions are not evident. However, affinities are abundant and if we can resist the temptation to read them as evidences of genetic linkages, their study can be fruitful.

In Seneca we find the same type of intuition of a universal order, a vast orchestration of numerous strands of causes and effects, that was foreshadowed in the great concept of *Rita* in Vedic poetry. As in Vedic thought, Marcus Aurelius sees the moral conscience of man, *Dharma*, as derived from this order or *Rita*. The stoicism of Aurelius was active, not passive. Like the *Gita*, it enjoined action and the fulfilment of duty without self-centred attachment to the merely material fruits of action.

In India, no philosophical system has been rejected as negative merely because it refused to accept the concept of a personal God. Only the rejection of the concept of *Dharma*, or moral imperative, led to failure in survival. Purva Mimamsa and the original Buddhist doctrine did not bother much about a personal deity, but both laid emphasis on *Dharma*. This being our background, we will have no difficulties in being wholly receptive to the great meditations of Lucretius. In a transient moment, Lokayata thought in India came to him. 'Who colours wonderfully the peacock, who makes the cuckoo coo so well? There is, in respect of these, no cause other than nature.' But the tragedy of Indian materialism is that it was pulled back from an investigation of the evolutionary power of nature because of its disastrously negative epistemological assumptions. The Lokayatikas accepted the authority of perception, but denied that it gave any evidence in support of causation, or a rational order in nature. Like Hume, centuries later, they denied that a causal relation between phenomena could ever be proved. Like Hume again, they denied that conscious life was a continuity, an integrated reality. With no order in nature to analyse or personal centre from which to analyse, the impulse towards the exploration of the outer and the inner world was stifled at birth. What could have evolved into positive science and philosophical vision stagnated as nihilist philosophy. Lucretius, on the other hand, never denied evolutionary power to matter. The atom, to him, had the inherent power of self-movement. Therefore he proceeds to trace the grand contour lines of the evolution of nature from primeval nebula to social systems and he sees the fulfilment of man in serene self-possession and love for all created things.

When evolution reaches the level of history, man is no longer its passive product, but the pilot of its further progression which will also be a self-evolution. Looking back on history, each mind makes its appraisal as to whether man has been the creator of history and can indeed be its creator. Tacitus was dealing with a sombre period in Roman history. We look through his eyes on a wrecked world viewed by him with a brooding fatalism. One of his many unforgettable phrases is the 'wrath of God against Rome' and occasionally he gives the impression that he believes in an unknown, capricious fate that drives men and states fatally onward to their destiny. The same sombre mood is seen in Kalhana when he contemplates the vast social decay in twelfth century Kashmir. But the flame of faith burned steadily in both, surrounded though it was by dense clouds of smoke. Kalhana made serene equanimity—*Santa Rasa*—the final note of his epic. This serenity did not mean lethargy or passivity. It involved detachment from egocentred drives, and altruistic action. Likewise, when Tacitus says that character is more important than government and that what makes a people great is not its laws but its men, his thought heaves itself up from the slough of despond and recovers its optimism about history.

But Virgil and Valmiki give us the grandest affirmation of man's responsibility in creating history. By a profound paradox, man rises to the deepest awareness of this responsibility when he lets himself become the willing instrument for helping in the realisation of a historic design conceived by a power far vaster than himself though he is part of it. Aeneas realises that all his travails and wanderings are steadily taking him nearer to the realisation of a historic purpose, the founding of a multinational state. Rama also feels that many developments, though seemingly wayward, unfair and unrelated—like the intrigues of Manthara and Kaikeyi and the abduction of Sita—are really orchestrated from deep below and are moving towards some grand finale: ridding the earth of the tyrannical order imposed by Ravana. The wanderings of Aeneas build up unifying associations over a vast realm so that they can contribute to the stability of the association of nationalities in the Roman state of Augustus. The wanderings of Rama and his alliance with the southern people have fulfilled the same purpose in the Indian tradition. And in the contrast between peace-loving, agricultural Ayodhya with its essentially democratic political system and the predatory regime of Lanka which sought to strengthen itself through war, subjection of other people and exaction of tribute, we have an astonishing parallel with Virgil's own ideas of the civilised polity.

Minor affinities are many. The moving scene of Jocasta going on an unsuccessful mission to the battlefield, in the *Thebaid* of Statius, to effect a reconciliation between her sons, recalls Kunti's visit to Karna on the eve of battle in the *Mahabharata*. The young Parthenopaeus in the same epic recalls Abhimanyu, condemned like him to die a heroic death at a tender age. The mood of the erotic poetry of Catullus and Ovid is shared by the bulk of the lighter poetry in Sanskrit and if Catullus has profounder moments of anguished introspection, we see them in Bhartrhari too. The ingenious servant who arranges the rendezvous in Plautus recalls the Vidushaka in the later Sanskrit comedy of Harsha and others and as in Harsha's *Priyadarsika* and *Ratnavali*, the heroines in Roman comedy also turn out in the end to be aristocratic girls kidnapped in childhood. Lastly, the robust Atellan comedy, memories of which persisted in rural Italy for centuries to give rise to the *Commedia dell'arte* of the sixteenth century, has fascinating parallels in our own folk forms, especially the Karyala of Simla which too works with only a skeleton plot outlined in advance, the dialogue being improvised during performance.

Lastly, we have the affinities between Horace's *Art of Poetry* and the tradition of Sanskrit poetics. Art, Horace insisted, is not raw feeling but feeling worked into perfect form. The basic principle in Bharata is the demand for the objectification of feeling in a creatively organised constellation of objective correlatives (the *Vibhavas, Anubhavas* and *Sanchari Bhavas*). Horace insists on clarity and the avoidance of long and pedantic words. Here he is like many critics in the Sanskrit tradition who demanded the quality of *Prasada* in poetry and preferred the Vaidarbhi style as against the Gaudi which went in for long compound words. Lastly, Horace wants the writer to study life and philosophy, for without observation and understanding, even a perfect style is an empty thing. We recall the great insights of Bharata. 'That drama alone deserves the world's sanction which is derived from human nature (*loka-svabhavajam*). The world is the authority (*pramana*) for the dramatic representation . . . Whatever sciences, morality, arts, behaviour derive from human nature, all that is the theme of drama. The reactivity (*bhava*) and behaviour (*cheshta*) of the world, of all that is mobile or immobile in it, have not been exhaustively determined in the texts. Great is the world's variety of behaviour. The dramatist must make the world the source of authenticity.'

The great works of the Romans have this authenticity and therefore universality. That is why we can proceed to assimilate their message and make it as much our heritage as the messages of the great minds of the Indian tradition itself.

KRISHNA CHAITANYA

Contents

1 Historical Background

In the mountainous, forested Italian peninsula, remains of human settlement go back to about thirty
centuries before Christ. The Old Stone Age culture
continued up to about 10,000 BC. Between 10,000
and 6000 BC a New Stone Age culture appeared.
Two tribes, known as the Liguri and the Siceli,
fashioned crude pottery, made tools with polished
stone, domesticated animals and lived by hunting
and fishing. About 2000 BC, northern Italy was
invaded by other tribes form central Europe, just as
Greece was invaded from the north by the ancestors
of the Greeks. A certain amount of admixture with
the Liguri and the Siceli was inevitable and this
fusion yielded the stock from which emerged the
various groups of the Roman race, like the Sabines
and the Latins. These people pastured flocks and
herds, tilled the soil, wove clothing, fired pottery,
made tools out of bronze and lived in settlements
with fortified walls and moats.

Seventeen miles from the mouth of the Tiber was a
place where the muddy, yellow river was narrow and

could therefore be forded by ferries. People from the north and south of the river used to meet here for exchanging their corn, cattle and other goods. The Roman tribes on the neighbouring seven hills took advantage of this by guarding the ford and demanding toll. In this way was born a small market village which was to develop later into Rome, one of the greatest cities of the world, which was destined to become the political centre of the ancient world during the Roman period, the religious centre of medieval Christianity, the cultural centre of the Renaissance and the mother city of a science of law which lives even today in the legal traditions of many contemporary states.

Legend has given us a romantic, alternative version of the founding of Rome. After the destruction of Troy by the Greeks, Aeneas, the Trojan hero and the son of Aphrodite (Venus), sailed to Italy and married the daughter of the Latin king. His descendant, Numitor, was expelled by an usurper, his sons killed and his daughter forcibly made into a priestess of Vesta, the goddess of virginity, so that she would not have any children. But, while sleeping on the bank of a stream, the breeze disarranged her robes, the god of war, Mars, fell in love with her and her two sons Romulus and Remus, whom the usurper ordered to be drowned, were brought up by a she-wolf. In the end they killed the usurper, restored their grandfather as king and built the city of Rome. There is no historical evidence to show that any group of Trojan immigrants participated in founding Rome, but the legend is very important, for it was accepted by Roman epic poetry, especially by Virgil.

During the first phase, the Romans were governed by a king or chieftain, who had great powers both in peace and war and was also chief judge and chief priest of the group. He was expected, however, to consult the nobles who formed a body called the Senate. Below the nobles were the common people and subsequent Roman history is the story of the repeated attempts made by this stratum of society to win their share in government.

But, something interfered with this political evolution in the beginning. About 800 BC a new flood of immigrants arrived, this time from Asia Minor, and established themselves in the northwest of Italy, right down to the Tiber, to the south of which lay the settlements of the Roman people. These invaders were known as the Etruscans and at the time of their appearance in Italy they had a superior culture, being more well-versed in the science of fighting than the Romans and possessing civilised traditions like painting and sculpture. The Etruscans captured

Rome and ruled over the Romans till 500 BC when
the nobles of the Roman people managed a success-
ful revolt. In 474 BC the weakened Etruscans
suffered a final defeat when their fleet was destroyed
by rival traders of the Greek colony in Sicily. This
strange people thus disappear from subsequent history. But, they left their influence on Roman dress,
state ceremonies, coinage and the system of education.

The defeat of the Etruscans is a very important event
in Roman history, for it saw the birth of the Roman
republic. The nobles did not restore Roman kingship in the place of Etruscan overlordship, but
divided the functions of kingship among supreme
state officials. The king's military command was
given to two officers called consuls. A new official
called the king of the ceremonies looked after
priestly functions of the earlier monarchy. Judges
took over the judicial powers. Of these new officers,
the consuls were the most important. They held
office only for a year. They were appointed by the
Assembly of the whole people and were responsible
to the Assembly when their term of office was over.
For guarding against a revival of monarchy, the
Assembly passed a law that any man who tried to
make himself king could be killed without trial.

We will need to study the evolution of the republic
in some detail for a fuller understanding of Roman

literature. Before we take that up, let us look at the growth of the great empire built up by the Romans. Even when the republic was young, it was threatened by wild tribes known as the Gauls (ancestors of the French people) from the north. In 390 BC the tribesmen managed to reach Rome and plundered and wrecked the city. But they were forced to withdraw by 300 BC. Originally, the Roman people had established themselves only in central Italy, in the plains watered by the Tiber. In the south of the peninsula were the old colonies established by the Greeks. A long conflict ensued, ending in the complete conquest of the Greek mainland and overseas provinces by 30 BC when Egypt, the last of the Greek states, fell to the Romans.

The Phoenicians, whose land was the Mediterranean coastal strip of Syria, were the greatest traders of antiquity and they had built up an empire in the wake of trade, as the British were to do in the eighteenth and nineteenth centuries. One of the most flourishing regions of the empire was Carthage in north Africa, right across the Mediterranean from south Italy. Sicily and even Spain formed part of the Phoenician empire. A long conflict ensued between Rome and Phoenician power for the control of the Mediterranean. Three long drawn out wars cover the period from 264 BC to 146 BC.

In Hannibal, Carthage produced one of the greatest generals the world has ever seen. He achieved the incredible task of crossing over from Africa to Spain with an army, one of the most formidable elements of which was a contingent of elephants trained for war, marching over the Alpine mountains and utterly destroying the Roman army in a pitched battle. But the Romans reorganised with indomitable courage and a long stalemate ensued, with the Romans avoiding pitched battles but harassing the enemy by guerilla tactics. A brilliant young general named Scipio attacked Carthage itself and thus forced Hannibal to leave Italy and return to defend his own land. There, in 202 BC, Hannibal was defeated and Rome took over all the warships of Carthage and annexed all her overseas territories like Spain, Corsica and Sardinia. Sicily had been wrested from Carthage earlier. A brokenhearted man, Hannibal lived on till 184 BC when, fearing capture and dishonour at the hands of the Romans on account of fresh troubles, he put an end to his life by drinking poison.

Though, at the close of the Second Phoenician war, between Scipio and Hannibal, Carthage itself was not annexed, the Roman nobles saw in the well-irrigated fields of north Africa the possibilities of obtaining rich estates for themselves, easily exploited by slave labour. Thus, the third and final war broke out and in

146 BC Carthage was burned, the majority of the people massacred and the surviving inhabitants enslaved. Phoenicia disappeared as a Mediterranean power.

Elsewhere also Rome gained victories. By 120 BC the Romans had conquered the land of the Gauls lying to the south of the Alps and also a part of the region occupied by the same tribes on the other side of the Alps. The next phase of expansion lasting up to 44 BC saw the defeat of Jugurtha, King of Numidia, and the annexation of his country which lay to the west of Carthage, Caesar's complete conquest of Gaul, the conquest of Dalmatia (the Adriatic coastal region of erstwhile Yugoslavia), of the north and south coasts of Asia Minor where King Mithridates proved for sometime a serious threat to Roman power, and of Cyrenaica, the region lying between Carthage and Egypt. By AD 14, Emperor Augustus brought the northward boundary of the empire up to the Danube and annexed Egypt, which, though it had been conquered earlier by Caesar, was threatening to remain outside the empire under Antony and Cleopatra. By AD 96, his successors had conquered Britain, northwest Africa and Thrace (the European portion of Turkey) and completed the conquest of Asia Minor. Emperor Trajan (AD 52–117) lastly, annexed Dacia (Romania and part of Hungary) and

Mesopotamia as well. Thus, at the height of its expansion, this great empire extended from Scotland to the Euphrates.

We can now return to the developments in the capital of this empire. In the first republican constitution, the people had sought to safeguard their rights by reserving the appointment of the consuls to the Assembly and making these highest executive officers of the Government answerable to the Assembly. Since wealth confers a lot of advantages in acquiring leadership, the consuls were, at first, always drawn from the nobility. In the day-to-day work, they were dependent on the advice of the nobility and their class interests were also the same. The Senate,thus,became very powerful. This led to agitation on the part of the commoners, both wealthy and poor. The Senate was a house of lords, membership being restricted by birth. Only the aristocratic families were admitted to it. The wealthy commoners resented this exclusion. The poorer people had even more serious grievances, for most of them were indebted to the nobles and the laws regarding defaults on debts were very repressive. The poorer commoners therefore demanded that these laws should be modified and that state lands and lands won in war should be distributed among the poor instead of being given free or sold at nominal prices to the nobles. The richer commoners wanted intermarriage with the nobility, so long prohibited by law.

Early in the fifth century, the commoners obtained Tribunes, officers elected by themselves and from their own class, whose function was to protect them from oppression at the hands of the nobles. These officers had the wide power of imposing their veto upon any law and any act of a magistrate which threatened the security of the commons. In 451 BC the commoners demanded and obtained a written codification of the laws of the state, which went a long way in assuring every citizen of equality before the law. The right of intermarriage was also obtained. Finally, in 367 BC the commoners managed to get a law enacted which helped them to control the executive power by the provision that oneConsul must—and bothConsuls might—be commoners.

Nevertheless, since wealth and political power confer great initial advantages in the economic struggle, the aristocratic class bitterly resisted this encroachment on their powers at every step. In the initial stages, Rome governed Italy like a colony, just as she governed her overseas domains. Italy was cut up into great estates owned by the nobles and worked by slaves. These estates went on increasing in size, for small farmers were drafted into the army for the numerous wars and during their absence their families sold or mortgaged the lands to the nobles. The Italian peasant fought and obtained the privileges of Roman citizenship. But when the citizenship was thus widened, the popular Assembly could not meet often, as it became a very huge and unwieldy body. Real power passed on to a smaller assembly of representatives of soldiers. This was a dangerous development, because the soldier became conscious of his potential power, and it foreshadowed the later development of military dictatorships. When the republic became the empire, the army sometimes used to auction the empire to the highest bidder, making the man who could give the maximum bribe to the soldiers the emperor.

The nobility had unrestricted powers over the slaves who worked in the farms. Killing slaves was not a crime. This absolute power created a blood-lust in the nobles. The commoners in the city were used to incredibly cruel amusements. Slaves and captured prisoners of war were thrown to hungry lions and the mobs got a hysterical delight in seeing the animals slaying and eating their human victims. The commoners also thus became used to violence of an extreme kind. It was no wonder, therefore, that the struggles between the aristocracy and the commoners became some of the bloodiest conflicts in history.

The Senate turned against its own members who pleaded for concessions to the commoners. Between 486 and 384 BC several senators were assassinated on the orders of the Senate itself, for wanting to distribute lands to the poor, to cancel debts or to distribute wheat at low, state-subsidised prices to the populace.

The period from 145 to 30 BC is one of revolution and protracted civil war. The revolution was started by the brothers Tiberius Gracchus and Caius Gracchus. They came from a very aristocratic family. Their mother, Cornelia, was the daughter of Scipio. But their aristocracy was one of ideals and not of power. Their father, Sempronius, had been the governor of Spain and whereas the senators who invariably became governors of the Roman provinces used to extort the maximum wealth for themselves, this man had won the affection of the whole country by his humane administration. A stoic philosopher, Blossius, was the counsellor of the brothers and they were well-read in the tradition of Greek democracy and the great age of Pericles.

Tiberius saw that the greed of the nobles was destroying the sturdy farmer class, the backbone of Italy. Cheap corn grown by slave labour on the estates of the senators, the biggest of them in the overseas provinces, undercut the produce of the

Italian farmer and ruined him. Prisoners captured in campaigns overseas were imported as slaves in large numbers and displaced the peasants in the countryside and the free workers in the towns. Roman society was being ruined by external plunder and internal slavery. In 133 BC Tiberius was elected Tribune and he announced his revolutionary programme. It was his intention to recover the land given to the nobles and distribute it among the poor. The same year he was killed. When his younger brother Caius asked permission to bury him, he was refused and the body was flung into the river Tiber. But Caius was resolved to go on with the work of his brother. He urged the distribution of subsidised corn to the commoners. The nobles pretended to agree but claimed that this should be left to them. Caius insisted that the State and not individuals would be responsible for the distribution. The conflict became violent once again and in 121 BC, Caius was also murdered. The Senate had offered a reward of its weight in gold for his head and the enterprising murderer filled it with molten lead to increase the weight. Tiberius had wanted to prevent the fresh growth of big estates by insisting that the redistributed lands should not be sold. The victorious nobles amended his provision and, as before, poverty stricken farmers began to sell their lands to the nobles and the big estates resumed their growth.

The next phase of the conflict shows the emergence of the political power of the army. It consisted mostly of commoners from the city and landless peasants from the rural areas. Their unconscious leanings were towards the people and against the nobility. But, primarily, they owed their loyalty to the commander under whom they served. The Roman soldier was entitled to booty from the defeated people and any commander who led them to many victories became their god. Marius, who had conquered a part of north Africa and driven back a dangerous inroad of Teuton (German) invaders in 102 BC, returned to Rome and toyed with the idea of seizing supreme political power. But he could not make up his mind as to which party to support. At first he supported Saturninus, a fiery revolutionary inspired by the ideals of the brothers Gracchus. But when the Senate ordered Marius to put down the revolution, he unthinkingly obeyed. Saturninus was killed, but the Senate, who knew of the vacillation of Marius, discarded him after making use of him and he died in gloomy retirement. Sulla was more unhesitatingly loyal to the Senate. Having put down a great revolt in Asia Minor and another in Italy, he came back victorious to Rome, supported the Senatorial party and in a great massacre in 81 BC, he executed five thousand of the popular party.

The conflict in Rome was between the wealthy nobles and the commoners who, even if they were poor, were free citizens. In the provinces was a vast population of men who had been free citizens of their native lands but were now slaves. They rose again and again against their oppressors. Violent slave revolts broke out in Etruria in 196 BC, in Apulia in 185, in Sicily in 139 and in Sinuessa in 133. In 73 BC occured a great rising of the slaves under Spartacus. This was suppressed with the greatest ferocity and the Roman trunk road to the provinces was lined with six thousand of their crucified bodies. Crassus, who defeated Spartacus, aimed at the dictatorship of Rome but he was killed in Persia. Then Pompey, having swept the pirates from the Mediterranean in a brilliant campaign of three months and having conquered Syria, returned to maintain an uneasy ascendancy at Rome in 61 BC till he was in turn defeated by Julius Caesar. A far greater man than his predecessors, he had trained a magnificent army in the course of nine years of fierce warfare in France and Britain and had come back to Rome as the champion of the popular party.

In the career of Pompey and Caesar, the army showed itself as the decisive factor in Roman political life. The law had required that returning generals should disband or disarm their troops at the gates of the city walls before entering the city. Pompey camped outside the city walls without disbanding his army and stood for election as consul. This was naked intimidation. When he became consul he compelled the Assembly to approve an extraordinary bill which gave him for three years, absolute control over all Roman fleets and over all persons within fifty miles of any Mediterranean shore. In effect this made him a king in everything but name and paved the way for Caesar's absolute dictatorship. Caesar even set up a statue of himself in a temple with the inscription 'The Unconquerable God.' Nevertheless, he was a great administrator and he initiated the task of establishing order throughout the empire which had been nearly ruined by the civil war. Before he could achieve much, however, he was assassinated in 44 BC. His nephew, Octavian, succeeded him as Augustus Caesar and stabilised the realm under his able rule from 31 BC to AD 14.

Gifted with good sense, moderation and practical capacity, Augustus never claimed the title of emperor. He was both Consul and Tribune of the people and thus could demand the loyalty of both the nobility and the people. He tried to preserve the prestige of the Senate as far as possible, but kept in his own hands effective control of the army and of all the important departments of the government. The overseas provinces were divided into two categories, those which were administered by the Senate and those which were governed by Augustus alone. So effective was his reorganisation that the Empire of Rome endured for four centuries after his death.

But, Rome had ceased to be a republic and dictatorship became the settled pattern, irrespective of whether the ruler tactfully pretended to derive his authority from the republican constitution or arrogantly claimed the title of emperor. During the first century after Christ, the emperors were often bad, but fairly capable. In the second century came a succession of hardworking, conscientious and efficient emperors, under whom there was internal peace and a considerable measure of prosperity. Then came two centuries of decay when the vitality of the Roman people was sapped in many ways till at last Rome fell to warlike tribes from the north.

The reasons for the fall of Rome are many. First of all, with the death of the republican spirit, martyrs for popular causes like the Gracchus brothers became rare and the concentration of land and the ruin of the sturdy peasant class went on at an accelerated pace. In the cities, crafts came to be organised on a guild basis, but people were forced by law to follow the profession of their parents and a caste system, as rigid as in India, thus came to be established.

The finest feature of the Roman character was a serious civic sense. By temperament the Roman was a stoic, but an active stoic, who never froze into passive indifference to the world, but resolutely pursued his duties, being indifferent only to the failures that occasionally confronted him. This strength of character was sapped by the habits of luxury fostered by the possession of an empire, of vast incomes from slave-worked estates in the conquered lands. The greatest tragedy was that this love of luxury led to race suicide. The rich, unmarried man was popular everywhere because all his acquaintances and friends hoped to be remembered in his will. Marriage and bringing up children went out of fashion and thus, gradually but steadily, the proportion of the old Roman stock in the empire decreased and the proportion of freed slaves, immigrants from other parts of the empire and tribals from beyond the frontiers who had joined the Roman army and later settled down at Rome, went on increasing.

In the early days, Roman religion had also contributed towards social solidarity. Roman religion was never inspired by any profound philosophy. It was a group ritual where all classes of the population came together and offered thanksgiving for harvest or victory in the battlefield. For the rest, the Roman was never exclusive and the gods of the conquered people were absorbed into the Roman pantheon. The old religion never took any side between the rich and the poor, republicanism and absolutism. But all this changed when the emperor became god and emperor-worship became the official religion. The earlier emperors had not worried about their divinity but derived their authority ultimately from the people. Even as late as in the beginning of the third century, when Ulpain, the jurist, enunciated the absolutist formula that 'the will of the emperor has the force of law', he added at once the democratic explanation that this was 'because the people confers upon him all its own sovereignty and power.' But in the next generation, Emperor Aurelian asserted his divine right and made emperor-worship the religion of the realm. This cult affected the vitality of the republic in two ways. A god cannot share his power with anybody else and the partnership of the Senate and emperor ended. Augustus had always taken the Senate into his confidence and the Senate also administered part of the empire. But the god emperor ignored the Senate and it became a mere corporation with powers only to look into the municipal affairs of Rome. Secondly, absolutism cannot tolerate freedom of thought and many emperors indulged in the practice of banishing philosophers and intellectuals.

The most dangerous development was the influx of the tribesmen from the frontier and beyond, into the Roman army. As the Roman stock dwindled due to race suicide, the ranks of the army had to be necessarily filled by these hardy people. They learned the value of freedom, discipline and the arts of war with the Roman army, and when they returned to their own people, they became the spearheads of the revolt against Rome. The Roman republic began its life by successfully resisting an attack by the Gauls in 390 BC. The Roman Empire fell because the restless tribes could no longer be checked by a society whose vitality had decayed. In AD 247, the Goths, a Germanic tribe coming from the north, crossed the Danube, destroyed the Roman province of Dacia (Romania and Transylvania) and killed the emperor Decius. In 410, Alaric the Goth captured Rome itself. These Goths later joined the Romans in resisting the attack of Attila, the terrible chieftain of the Mongolian Huns, in AD 451. Fresh waves of Goths pillaged Rome in 455 and in 476, the last Roman Emperor resigned his throne, to be succeeded by a Gothic chieftain, named Theodoric, as King of Italy. The great city ceased to be the capital of the Roman Empire. Though it revived later as the capital of a Christian Europe, in which the violent tribes were gradually tamed into civilised life, that story has to be postponed to a later volume.

Though ancient Rome perished, it lives today in innumerable prolongations. The languages of many parts of the empire evolved from the spoken Latin that was current in those regions. Italian, French, Spanish, Portuguese and Romanian are languages evolved in this manner and in the case of the other languages also, Latin has left a rich legacy of words. Rome was also the first among the ancient civilisations to realise the dream of a world state. The concept itself had been anticipated in the dreams of the Greek stoics and in the achievements of Alexander. But Greek stoicism was passive and there was no urge to realise the dream through strenuous effort. As for Alexander, he was not granted the length of life to consolidate his astonishing victories. In the case of Rome itself, the concept of the world state was not realised without a struggle. A world state implies a world citizenship. Many difficulties had to be overcome for realising this ideal. The commoners had to fight for admission into the Senate, originally reserved for the hereditary nobility. Then the Italian peasant had to win the privileges of Roman citizenship. Later the people of the overseas provinces had to fight for the same rights. In AD 212 Emperor Caracalla promulgated a constitution by which all freeborn members (as distinct from slaves) of the communities of the empire were granted Roman citizenship, which made them all possessors of equal rights before the law.

It is in the clear definition of these rights that Roman legal genius gave its richest legacy to humanity. The Greeks had laid the foundation of constitutional law and shown how freedom may be best secured to all citizens through a democratic form of government. But, in day-to-day life, freedom is more a matter of delicate balancing of the rights of individuals in disputes among themselves and between the citizen and the state. We owe to Rome this clear formulation of civil and criminal law. At first, it was an archaic system suited only to a limited agricultural community. But when the empire expanded and Roman administration came into contact with many different peoples, a more efficient merchant law slowly evolved. Since this legal system had to be applied to the vast stretch from Scotland to the Euphrates, it had to be flexible and comprehensive, assimilating different traditions. Though this legal system was largely forgotten in the ages that followed the breaking up of the empire by tribes, it endured in France and Italy in corrupted form, until it was rediscovered and reapplied in the later medieval and modern periods. The American and French Revolutions were inspired by Roman definitions of the rights of the individual when they established their Republics. Today, Roman law forms the basis of the legal traditions of many states of the world.

The world rule of the later emperors was corrupt and led to the disappearance of freedom and the decay of civilisation. But we must not forget that the worship of the emperor as god replaced the numerous local cults and made it easier for Christianity to establish an empire ruled, not by a man claiming to be a god, but by a church ruling in the name of God. This was a great experiment. The fact that this order also fell later into corruption and gave way to the Reformation in the sphere of religion and the rise of national states in the sphere of politics, should not make us forget its achievements. These achievements were very much helped by the fact that the Romans had built up a multi-racial empire in the first place and secondly, unified its traditions under a common administration and later under a divine emperor.

The Romans were a practical people and therefore, in the realm of the arts, they did not make original contributions. Greece had already paved the way in architecture, sculpture and painting and from the Greek colonies of south Italy, the Romans came to know of these traditions. But, with the wealth of the world behind her, Rome could do everything on a much more magnificent scale than Greece. The medieval cathedral is built on the pattern of the Roman temple. She built triumphal arches and decorated them with ornamental sculptural motifs. Her portrait sculptures have an extraordinary realism. Her fresco paintings have a large spaciousness. Her wealth enabled many industrial arts to flourish.

Now that we know something of the Roman people, we can proceed to enjoy their literature.

2 Epic Poetry

There is some indirect evidence to show that it was the custom of the old Romans, at the end of a banquet, to sing the glory of their ancestral heroes in narrative verses, accompanied by the flute. This oral tradition, however, has not survived and the literary epic of later times was modelled on the Greek tradition.

In 272 BC, Tarentum, the Greek colony in south Italy, fell to the Romans. Andronicus, a Greek enslaved in this campaign, was brought to Rome and became the teacher of the children of a Roman nobleman. He was freed later and was destined to become the teacher, not only of his pupils, but also of the entire Roman people, for it was he who initiated a literary movement in the Latin language. He translated Homer's *Odyssey* into Latin verse and wrote dramas also. Only a few fragments of the *Odyssey* have survived and their literary quality is not very high. Nevertheless, the translation introduced the Roman people to a great work of imaginative literature, the world of the Greek heroes, greater than ordinary men, yet profoundly human, passionate and daring, courageous in the face of tragic vicissitudes.

This beginning of Latin literature is symbolical of its entire life and growth. In every literary form and tradition, we can see a derivation from Greek sources. But the genius of many of the Roman writers made the final outcome individual and personal, mirroring Roman life and not Greek memories in their content, as distinguished from their form. In the epic tradition, we must note that unlike the Mesopotamians or the Greeks, the Romans had no epic poem dating back to the racial infancy and surviving for long in oral tradition before being written down. Rome, here, has greater affinity with Egypt where the epic tradition developed out of the imaginative rehandling of contemporary or recent history.

This truth is brought out by the literary career of Naevius which followed that of Andronicus within a few years. He was an Italian from Campania in south Italy, who fought in the first Punic (Phoenician) War and was an ardent champion of the commoners in their struggles against the aristocrats, who imprisoned and finally banished him. A fiery, enthusiastic genius, Naevius felt that the war in

which he had just fought was as great a theme as the
Greek attack on Troy. So, although he took the epic
form from Homer, he wrote about the Punic War.
Since Greek legends seemed to be the source of all
epics, he linked his poem to the ancient story by
making Trojan refugees the founders of the city of
Rome. This might have been pure invention on his
part or such a legend might have been current in
southern Italy. But Virgil accepted the legend and
made a great epic on the theme.

Virgil (70–19 BC) wrote other poems besides his epic
on Aeneas, the Trojan hero. Since these other works
also have something of the grandeur of epic ideal
and vision, we may discuss all his compositions here.
This will enable us to study the growth of his mind
in a complete, unified account.

The greatest of the Roman poets was not perhaps of
pure Roman stock. He was born near Mantua in
north Italy, in a region long occupied by the Gauls
south of the Alps. Technically he was a Gaul by
birth, for this region was granted Roman citizenship by Caesar only twenty-one years after Virgil
was born. The Gauls were of Celtic stock and it is
significant that in place of the hard, sturdy strength
of the Roman character, we find in Virgil a grace,
tenderness and mysticism that suggest a Celtic strain.

His father had bought a riverside farm and had taken up bee keeping. So great was the influence of this early environment that, though Virgil had his education in the cities of Cremona, Milan and Rome, he did not choose a public career but returned to his farm. But he was not allowed to live there in peace. In the civil wars, this region had sided with the enemies of Octavian and therefore large tracts of land in this area were confiscated and distributed to discharged soldiers. Virgil's farm was also taken over in this manner. However, Pollio, the governor of southern Gaul, took a liking for the young man and gave him his patronage. Virgil's first volume, the *Eclogues* or *Pastoral Poems*, was written during this phase.

These poems were inspired by Theocritus, the Sicilian poet who originated the Greek pastoral tradition. In them, idealised shepherds sing their songs against a dreamlike background of mountain, woods and streams. Some of them are single songs by individual shepherds. Some are in dialogue form. Others are singing matches in friendly rivalry. Most of the themes are traditional: love, lamentation for parting or absence, the friendly banter of the rustics. The pastoral form has always stood in danger of becoming artificial. But these poems breathe sincerity, for Virgil cherished the memories of his early years and was passionately fond of the rural landscape and life. His genius gave a new music to language and all those who read the poems marvelled at their sweet, flawless diction and the genuine strength of the love of nature and humanity that inspired them. Pastoral poetry was also rescued from its tendency to withdraw from life by Virgil who wrote with feeling on contemporary events. Thus, the confiscation of lands and the sufferings of the peasants also figure in these poems, rendered in moving verse.

The fourth poem in this volume of ten poems is one of the most famous in the world. It was addressed to Pollio when a son was born to the poet's patron. The poet celebrates the birth of a child during whose time the Golden Age of peace and innocence will come again. A prophetic power stirs beneath the surface in this poem. Within a decade Octavian would assume the title Augustus and establish order throughout the realm, so long ruined by civil war. The Augustan Age was referred to as the Golden Age of Rome, for in every way it brought the empire to its climax of prosperity. In the middle ages, Christian writers saw in this poem a prophetic intuition of the coming of Christ and therefore, although the Church discouraged the study of pagan writers, Virgil was often exempted as a pagan prophet of the birth of Christ.

Whatever the specific prophetic reference of the poem, it will have a perennial appeal, for it voices the permanent longing of the human race for a happier earth, untouched by the quarrels and miseries that seem to pursue history like avenging furies. Reading it, we feel lifted up with Virgil in a prayerfull anticipation of a great advent. There may yet be another war but it will be a war to end wars, 'one final war, with another great Achilles storming a last Troy.' Then the last age will come, the great circle of the centuries will begin again and the great months begin their march when we shall lose all trace of the old guilt and the world will learn to forget fear under a prince of peace who shall command that all swords shall be beaten into ploughshares. Then will the entire landscape be covered with the gold of ripening corn. We can understand the passionate longing of the poet for a new order, when he contemplated the war ruined landscape of his beloved Mantuan countryside and, since we live under even graver threats, our own hearts soar up with this vision.

The pastoral poems brought the poet fame and won for him the friendship of Maecenas, the Chief Minister of Augustus. The next volume was written under imperial patronage. The title and background of this work would seem to suggest, at first sight, a most prosaic and uninteresting performance. Augustus was attempting to revive Italian agriculture, long ruined by civil war, and Maecenas encouraged Virgil to compose a poem in support of the Emperor's agrarian policy. The result was the *Georgics* or *Poem on Agriculture*.

Those who marvel about what agricultural revival has to do with poetry should realise what it meant to the life of the nation and remember the integrity and capacity of the poet who wrote the poem. The Roman peasant had been ruined by the growth of large, slave-worked estates in the overseas provinces. On occasions when Rome's enemies had succeeded in a naval blockade of her communications with the overseas regions, Rome had faced starvation and surrender. Such crises reminded Rome that if the sturdy economic system of the past, which was essentially agricultural, and based on small, independent farmers, had not been allowed to go into ruin, the nations's life would not have been in peril. The ruin of the peasant farmer also indicated a profound moral decay of the nation. For, the more complete the ruin of the small, middle class farmers, the more powerful became the nobles who took over their lands. Increased wealth gave increased political power which the nobles ruthlessly used to entrench themselves in their privileged position and to resist a democratic sharing of civic rights with the people. Further, the peasants, driven out from their lands, drifted to the city and became members of the anonymous mob, hating work, living on subsidised food, trained in violence by the cruel amusements of the city whose favourite spectacle was the slaying of slaves and prisoners of war by wild animals. Such a mob was a threat from below, as the landowning nobility was a threat from above, to the democratic way of life. The great task that confronted Augustus was first the redistribution of the huge estates and then inducing peasants from the city to go back to the rural areas. Thus we see that agricultural reform here meant the economic as well as moral rebirth of the nation.

On the face of it, the volume is a practical guide to farming. The stated topics of the four sections of the work are technical details concerning field crops, orchards and vineyards, flocks and herds, and bee-keeping. When we come to Roman lyrical poetry we shall see that the bulk of it is urban in its sentiment, affinities and cultural background. If a poet of this type had been commissioned to write this poem, the result would have been as prosaic as anyone would expect the theme to be. But the rural life had shaped Virgil's sensibilities. In Greece, the high sincerity of Hesiod yields enduring poetry from the theme of the rhythm of work in the rural areas. Virgil had more imagination, idealism and craftsmanship than Hesiod and, therefore, the result is a great poem in which Virgil's ideal of human life as part of universal nature blends with his concept of the holiness of word and the greatness of Rome and unfolds in exquisite music against the beauty of the Italian countryside.

Virgil begins his poem with an account of primitive life when man lived by hunting and agriculture was unknown. Then civilisation began to evolve. 'All things were overcome by labour and by force of bitter need.' The hunting and nomadic life changed to the settled life of patiently tilling the earth. The earth was a bountiful mother but she rewarded only those who worked. 'Up, then! while the soil is still heavy with the winter damp, in the very first months of the year, let your stout bulls turn it over, so that the sods may be baked by summer with its full suns.' Then, in outlining the cycle of the seasons, the poem becomes like Kalidasa's *Ritu Samhara*. Summer and autumn follow with days so crowded with work that they seem like brief flickers of light in a continuous night, the golden dawn almost immediately followed by reddening evening come to light her final stars. Then come the late autumnal storms, when the whole atmosphere explodes in thunder, the enormous earth quivers, the rivers filled by the lashing rain rise and roar and seethe in their spuming beds and, over the desert wastes of sea, tempests rage in unabated fury. The storms cleanse the skies of dust and clouds and the stars twinkle with a brighter lustre. Then comes the winter and the days slow down pleasantly by the fireside, while the peasant women sing old melodies to the rhythm of the shuttle. The poem is studded with unforgettable pictures of the countryside. 'Unceasingly the year lavishes fruit or young of the flock or sheaf of the corn blade and loads the furrow and overflows the granary with increase. The oil seed is crushed in the presses. Autumn brings his manifold fruitage and high up on the sun-drenched rocky ground the grapes ripen.' Virgil seems to have believed that social justice could prevail only in such a society where men realised that work was the sacred duty of everybody. Only work could keep men away from quarrels and allow civilisation to ripen and mature, accumulate precious memories. Human labour clears the forests, makes settled life possible and brings in its wake all the achievements of peace: 'Here is an eternal spring, interrupted only by summer. Twice in the year the flocks bear young, twice the tree gives apples. There are no tigers. No scaly serpent drags itself in coils. But there are fine cities, and mighty works, and little towns set on sheer rocks by the hands of men, and rivers flowing under ancient walls.'

In the pastoral poems Virgil sang about the Golden Age. In this work, he shows how it can be established by man. Work is the secret of the triumph of man and the guarantee of his further progress. Work is a moral discipline. The Roman aristocrat might disdain to drive a plough. But every feature in the rhythm of work close to nature has a secret but significant contribution to make to the development of personality. And, out in the fields, where man participates in the myriad forces of nature and assists in the sacred mystery of growth and renewal of life, the soul, more readily than in the city, perceives the presence of creative life, and is deepened with religious intuition, humility and reverence. This is the great humanistic message of a poem whose context of origin had seemed so prosaic.

We now come to the great epic poem, *Aeneid* or the story of Aeneas, on which Virgil worked during the last ten years of his life. He died before he could revise it and in his will he had left instructions that the manuscript should be destroyed. But Augustus overruled this and published the poem which soon became the national epic of Rome. There are plenty of classical derivations in the structure of the epic.

As in Homer's *Iliad*, a war—for the domination of Rome between the Trojan immigrants and the Latin people—is the climax of the epic. As in Homer's *Odyssey*, Aeneas has to wander for many years before he reaches his destination. The gods take sides in the dispute and the hero visits the land of the dead as in the Greek epics. But all these borrowed elements acquire the power of a new intimation. In fact, Virgil was creating an epic of an altogether new type, an epic which was a vehicle of his lofty ideas about Rome's historic destiny.

Virgil had enough clear vision not to exaggerate the virtues and achievements of the Roman character. He saw that there were many fields in which the Roman people showed no special aptitudes. But he believed—and history has vindicated the belief—that Rome had a genius for government. In a passage in the *Aeneid*, Virgil wrote: 'Others shall beat out the breathing bronze to softer lines, I believe it well; they shall draw living lineaments from the marble; arguments shall be more eloquent on their lips; their pencils shall portray the pathways of heaven and tell the stars in their arising. But be thy charge, O Roman, to rule the nations in thine empire; this shall be thine art, to lay down the law of peace, to be merciful to the conquered and beat the mighty down!' Earlier to Virgil, another poet,

4

Ennius, (239–169 BC) had written an epic history of
Rome, the message of which was that the 'Roman
state stands through its ancient morals and its great
men'. This poem had also begun with Aeneas. But
only fragments have survived and they do not have
the moral fervour of Virgil's poem.

The hour of doom comes for Troy. The great, dread,
unseen presences of the gods, who had decreed its
fall, throng the city. The remnants of the Trojan
heroes perish in the last battle and even the old King
Priam who had seen all his sons die in the field is not
spared by fate. 'The great corpse lies upon the shore,
a severed head, a trunk without a name.' The shade
of great Hector appears to the Trojan prince Aeneas
and asks him to leave Troy and prophesies that after
many wanderings over the sea he shall establish a
great city. We at once note the difference between
this epic and its Greek models. The destiny of
individuals, of Hector and Achilles, dominates the
design of the *Iliad*. Virgil's concern is the destiny not
of a man but a nation, for from the wanderings of
Aeneas came 'the Roman race and the lofty walls of
Rome.' There is another lofty intimation in this
part of the story. Hector's shade gives the images of
the household gods of Troy to Aeneas to safeguard
him during his wanderings. But he dares not touch
them with his bloodstained hands. This fine thought

brings out Virgil's hatred of wars. Aeneas requests his father Anchises to take charge of them. This reflects the Roman tradition which regarded the family as a sacred institution and insisted on due reverence to the head of the family from the younger members.

So, Aeneas builds a fleet and sets out with his father and son and a few followers. The voyage was long and filled with peril. For seven years they wandered, driven by fate from land to land. Besides providing the occasion for long poetic narratives necessary for reaching the dimensions of an epic, Virgil had a higher purpose in mind in the descriptions of these wanderings. By his visits, Aeneas, the founder of Rome, builds up associations, very much earlier than the establishment of the empire or even of Rome itself, with the Mediterranean lands destined later to become part of the Roman world state. The poem thus becomes the common possession of not only the Romans but also of the other peoples associated with her in a common government.

After they reached Sicily, Anchises died. Saddened by his loss, but hopeful that their journey was almost over, they put out to sea again. But the goddess Juno, who dislikes Aeneas, since he is the son of her rival Venus, sends a storm and the fleet is wrecked on the coast of Africa. Here, Dido, a widowed Phoenician queen who had escaped from her original city of Tyre, destroyed by enemies, was founding the city of Carthage. She befriends the Trojans. Actually, Virgil's epic begins with the storm that drives them into Carthage and the earlier part of the story is given in retrospect. This was because the poet wanted his poem to begin straightaway at a point of greatest interest in the fortunes of his hero.

The story of the stay in Carthage is a moving, tragic idyll with profound meanings hidden in its depth. Dido, herself an exile from Tyre, beginning a new life after defeat in war and wanderings, sympathises with the Trojans and gives them a warm welcome. She entertains them to a feast and the song sung by her harpist at the banquet gives a veiled suggestion that Aeneas is going to forget, for some time at least, that he is a man with a historic mission and be content to be just a man with his instincts and emotions. The harpist sings of the beginnings of life, of beasts and men, the daily toil of the sun, moonrise and moonset, of lightings and storms, the cycle of winter and spring. Along with the animals, man is a part of nature. To the extent that man lives wholly at the level of nature, he creates no history, just as vegetation and the animal world have no history. Under the Carthaginian skies, Aeneas for a time subsides to the level of a man unconscious of his mission. Dido and Aeneas are drawn together and consummate their union in the depths of a forest. Their union has no witnesses except the earth and sky. Lightnings are the marriage torches, the only attendant is the air, and the unseen wood nymphs alone sing the marriage chants.

But, the idyll is not destined to last. The consciousness of his mission awakens in Aeneas and he announces his decision to resume the journey. He sheds tears for Dido but he cannot abdicate his historical purpose. The poet describes how Dido spent the last night before the day broke which was to see the Trojans sail away from Carthage: 'Night fell. Weary creatures took quiet slumber all over earth, and woodland and wild waters had sunk to rest. Now the stars wheel midway on their gliding path, now all the country is silent, and beasts lay couched asleep under the still night. But not so the distressed queen; nor does she allow sleep to bring peace to her tired eyelids or restless heart. Her pain redoubles and her love swells to renewed madness. . .' When dawn broke and the sea shore was empty and the Trojan ships were about to sail, she stabs herself to death and the Trojans, from far out in the sea, see the flames rising from her funeral pyre.

This tragic episode is used by Virgil to fulfil many hidden purposes. It reveals the forgivable weakness of his hero and therefore shows him to be profoundly human. On the other hand, in the decision to take farewell from Carthage, Aeneas becomes a conqueror of his own inclinations, acquiring a stoic courage which Virgil believed indispensable for men who created history. Aeneas pleads that he never married Dido in holy wedlock according to the prescribed rites. This does not seem to be a very noble attitude, but it does reduce his own guilt, for the Romans attached great importance to the sacredness of the family and Aeneas did not violate it. Dido herself was modelled on the Medea of the Greek writer Apollonius and has something of the passionate impetuousness of her prototype. When her husband died, she had taken an oath never to marry again, but to dedicate herself to the building of a new city for her people. She forgets her vows to her husband and, in killing herself, she forgets her duties towards her people. Virgil also uses Dido's death to strengthen the epic quality of his poem, for Dido prophesies an avenger from Carthage, who shall bring misery to Rome. Hannibal was this avenger. This leads in turn to Virgil's lofty statesmanship. In the Punic wars, Rome had totally destroyed Carthage. Rome could claim that this was just vengeance for Hannibal's attack. But, in suggesting that Hannibal himself came as the result of the curse of discarded Dido, Virgil was inducing the Romans to

reconsider the whole issue. On the site of the Phoenician city of Carthage, cursed and deserted more
than a century before, Augustus had ordered a new
city to be built, as capital of Roman Africa. Virgil
did not want the people of this new city to retain
memories of the terrible wrongs of the Punic wars.
The story of Dido and Aeneas would induce them
to believe that the spirits of the dead lovers had
reunited and become the guardians of their new city.
'Trojans and Phoenicians: I shall deem them as one,'
Dido had said when she welcomed the wanderers
and had hoped that they would settle down in
Carthage. This was not to be in her life time. But, in
cleansing the atmosphere of tragedy and cruel de-
sertion that hung over the old site, by his delicate
handling of the old story, Virgil was working towards his ideal of Rome as a commonwealth of many
peoples.

Aeneas resumes his wanderings. The end of his
mission is not in sight and Venus, the mother of the
hero, complains to Jupiter about the unjust sufferings meted out to her son. But Jupiter comforts her
with a narration of his ultimate success and the great
destiny in store for the state Aeneas will establish.
Such a foretelling by the gods belongs to the familiar
apparatus of Greek epic poetry. There is a subtle but
important difference. In the Greek epics, gods seem

to decree the fate of men, and the events of their lives obey this irresistible fate. But in Virgil, fate is not such an inexorable preordaining. Even if events are fated, they come to pass through human will and action. Man thus becomes a creator of his historic destiny, whether it is achievement or failure. Jupiter says:

> *Each man's acts shall bring*
> *Him toil or luck. Jupiter's rule is one for all.*
> *The Fates shall find a way.*

Here fate is not a sombre preordaining but a vast fulfilment that works through the conflict and concord of many forces, a pattern that ultimately emerges from the play of many energies among them the energy of the human will. Therefore, Aeneas cannot let things drift in the hope that the momentum of decreed events will by itself take him up to the crest of history. He has to identify himself with a purpose higher than his own individual destiny and irrespective of the weariness the task brings him. 'I seek not Italy by choice,' were his parting words to Dido: not by personal choice, but in obedience to a historic purpose, higher than any individual. When, during his wanderings, he stops to pay homage at the tombs of ancient heroes, he becomes envious of their final rest: 'Your rest is won. No seas have you to plough. Nor is your task to seek a land that moves for ever backward.' But he knows he cannot rest and that all dangers have to be confronted to reach the ultimate goal. 'Through many dangers, many a change and chance, we move to the destined land.'

The Trojans sailed northward from Carthage and landed near Cumae on the west coast of Italy. Here Aeneas sought out an ancient woman prophet who lived in a cave nearby. With her to guide him, he descended into the land of the dead, where he found his father among the blessed. In the words of Anchises to his son, Virgil seems to set forth his own philosophy. There is a world spirit that pervades the universe and gives life to all things. An inner breath sustains earth and heaven and the watery wastes of the sea, the moon's bright sphere and the gigantic stars. Mind moves matter, throughout the mighty frame of the universe. Platonic mysticism and stoic pantheism have inspired Virgil here and his doctrine is capable of acceptable restatement today. Though divine, the spirit's tranquillity is disturbed when it is united with the matter out of which the body is composed. Emotions and passions arise within it. It loses its original purity and it has to return to earth after death for further trials. This doctrine of reincarnation is derived from Pythagoras and the whole thought has affinities with Indian speculations.

What is important to us is that Virgil believes that final release can come only through conduct free from passions.

Anchises also shows his son the souls of the great Romans yet to be and Aeneas stands spellbound watching the long line of Roman souls waiting to be reborn. In a later vision, Venus shows him the battle of Actium (31 BC) where Octavian defeated Antony who had wanted to break Egypt away from the Empire, and also the other triumphs of Octavian when he assumed supreme control under the name Augustus. These visions fulfil a more pointed structural function in the epic. Unlike other epics, Virgil's poem was written by a close student of current history, who could clearly see the ideals which alone could guarantee future historical greatness to Rome and who wanted to project these ideals back so that they would emerge as the fruits of a long and continuous development. Augustus himself was believed to be a descendant of Aeneas. Aeneas, in the poem, reflects the character of Augustus and the enlightened policy of that statesman towards Carthage was given a great imaginative and moral support in the epic. The vision of future leaders of the Roman people and of Roman achievements helped further to knit past and present into a continuous development. Virgil used yet another device for this purpose in his description of the mighty shield of Aeneas. For, it is ornamented with scenes depicting the critical phases through which Rome would successfully pass in subsequent history. The last of these scenes depicts the despotism of Antony and Cleopatra from which Augustus saved Rome.

From Cumae, the Trojan fleet sailed north along the coast of Italy and came to a halt at the mouth of the river Tiber. Latinus, the king of that country, had an only daughter (Lavinia) who, an oracle had predicted, would marry a foreign prince. Latinus prepares to give his daughter to Aeneas but Turnus, a former suitor of the princess, calls the people to arms against the Trojans. Virgil has handled the delineation of the character of Turnus with great delicacy. He is courageous and patriotic. But historic destiny, which has grander plans for Rome, sweeps him away. At the hour of his death he has a dim intuition of the vaster purpose for which he has been sacrificed. He feels that his defeat and death are due, not so much to the superiority of the Trojans, but to the purpose of the gods regarding the destiny of the land. He has done his duty according to his rights and he leaves the world without regrets or self-pity:

> *Is death a sorrow? Spirits of the dead,*
> *Be kind to me, since Heav'n has turned away.*

> *A soul unstained, unblamed, I shall go down*
> *In naught unworthy of my mighty sires.*

In the conduct of the war, Aeneas always shows that his only aim is the swift restoration of peace. When a young warrior of the enemy forces dies by his hand, Aeneas looks on the face of the young man, the pity of it all overwhelms him and he stretches his hand as if to bring back the dead body to life. When the enemy sends their envoys, seeking permission to bury the dead, he is willing to grant much more than that:

> *Peace for the dead and slain in war you ask.*
> *I'd grant it gladly to the living too.*

But peace comes only with the death of Turnus. The goddess Juno has been vigorously aiding the Latins against the Trojans. At last she consents to the victory of the Trojans if certain conditions are obeyed. These conditions are of great importance, for her essential demand is that the Trojans and the Latins are to live in peace, not as conquerors but as equals. She wants Troy to be forgotten and the Trojans to adopt Rome as their motherland. The Latin people should not be asked to change their names, dress or language. The two races are to fuse together completely and create the Roman race of the future. In these touches, again, Virgil's poetic inspiration is equal to the statesmanship of Augustus. After winning the civil wars, Augustus gave complete amnesty to the people who had fought against him and his great mind dreamt of a multi-racial state, solidly united under an impartial administration.

The greatness of *Aeneid* lies in the fact that, though cast in an antique mould, the poem breathes a totally new spirit. In Homer, we go back to legendary epochs when men were godlike in their strength. Here, at every phase in the unfolding of the story, we see a contemporary significance. The hero is human and nearer to us because of his failings. The heroes of Homer sought glory. Aeneas sees the emptiness of individual fame. The old heroes achieved marvels of heroism in battle. Aeneas has a greater task: to fight his own inclinations and weariness and persist in his historic task. And this historic task was not confined within the limits of a narrow patriotism, but looked forward to the founding of a world state where all races would be equal.

[handwritten margin note: Aeneid can be related more to the reader than the Homeric epic]

In 19 BC, while travelling in Greece, Virgil suffered a sunstroke. He was immediately taken home, but died shortly after his ship reached Italy and was buried near Naples. For a long time, his tomb was revered as a sacred shrine. Today we do not know the site of his mortal remains. But his spirit has won a permanent home in the hearts of all who can be moved by greatness of imagination and idealism.

Epic poetry continued to be written after Virgil. But it lost the greater vision of Virgil and reverted to the older models which preferred the external trumult and the fluctuating fortunes of war to the internal self-conquest and steadiness in the fulfilment of historic purposes. Nevertheless, many of the epics have literary value and, coming after Virgil, they could not fail to be touched with greater intimations, on occasions at least.

Silius Italicus, who was born in AD 26, wrote the longest of the surviving Roman epics. It is entitled *Punica* and its theme is the second Phoenician war, during which Hannibal nearly destroyed Rome. Like the old epics, this poem also shows a close participation of gods in human affairs. But Silius was not able to understand the subtlety with which Virgil handled this old convention. In Virgil, even the gods are mere symbols of a providence larger than they. But in the present poem, the gods revert to their older role, merely adding to the crowds of participants in the conflict. Juno reappears in her old role as the enemy of Rome. It is she that kindles Hannibal's hatred for Rome, causes the outbreak of the war, and disguised as a lake-god, spurs him on to Rome.

Nevertheless, the characters in the poem are cast in a heroic mould. When Hannibal defeats and kills a Roman general, he begins to feel the pity of war. Looking on his brave enemy, he cries: 'Go, Rome's glory, where the souls of those, whom valour and noble deeds make great, may go. You have won great glory by your death. As for us, fortune still tosses us to and from in weltering labour and forbids us to see what chance the future has in store.' During Hannibal's long occupation of Italy, he was held at bay by the guerilla tactics of Fabius, who never offered pitched battle but continuously harassed the Carthaginian army. In his description of Fabius, Silius shows his capacity for effective and lovely imagery: 'Nothing Fabius attempts, but has some guile in it. He weighs every scheme, sharpens his mind and ever attacks at unexpected times and places, even as the gleam of water lit by the sun's radiance dances through a house quivering and the reflected beam of light goes wandering and lashes the roof with tremulous reflection.'

Silius, even in the midst of the tumult of war, felt that such bloody conflicts withheld from man the fruits of civilisation which only peace could assure.

He praises Marcellus, the Roman conqueror of Syracuse, for showing the greatest clemency towards that city. In this campaign, Archimedes (287– 212 BC), the greatest experimental scientist of antiquity, who had even invented a steam engine, though it was never put to industrial use, was killed by soldiers as he was working on a mathematical problem. Silius shows Marcellus as shedding tears over such a loss at the hour of his conquest. Finally, he has enough understanding of history to see that Hannibal's occupation of Italy was really a blessing in disguise, as it steeled Roman character for further trials, and he projects this insight into the future: 'And the time shall come when Rome, the greatest thing in all the world, shall be yet more ennobled by her woes.'

Lucan burnt out his life quickly, at the very young age of twenty-five, in AD 65. He was the nephew of the philosopher Seneca and like him, was born in southern Spain. At twenty-one, he won a prize in one of the poetic contests which Emperor Nero, who fancied himself to be a poet, used to organise. Nero loved flattery, and the title of the poem was *In Praise of Nero*. But when Nero found that Lucan's poetic talents outshone his own, the jealous and eccentric emperor ordered him not to write any more. Lucan joined a conspiracy against Nero, was arrested, broke down and revealed the names of the other conspirators, even, we are told, of his mother. When Nero condemned him to death, his courage revived and he summoned his friends to a feast, ate with them heartily, then opened his veins and bled to death reciting his own poetry. We should forgive his lapses remembering his extreme youth and recognise the talents of a high order which went into the creation of his epic poem, entitled the *Civil War*.

It deals with the conflict between Caesar and Pompey and a central episode is the battle of Pharsalia which saw the final decline of Pompey's fortunes. Nero was a descendent of a general who had fought and died in this war as the ally of Pompey. And Lucan, who began the poem under Nero's patronage but completed it after the estrangement, is at first partial to Pompey. Nevertheless, his poetic imagination does not follow the dictate of his intellect and its bias due to ambition regarding career. Very revealing is his indirect comparison of Pompey to a huge tree outliving its time: 'The roots, once mighty, hold it no more. Weight is its only stay. Its naked limbs bespeak its past glories and if it continues to cast a sheltering shade for a little while more, it is not by its wealth of foliage, for the leaves have withered away, but by its massive trunk.'

Against his bias, Caesar's greatness comes to live again in the poem. Caesar had 'the unresting soul, the high resolution, that shut out every thought but victory.' He was so thorough that he felt 'nothing was done while anything remained to do.' Caesar 'compelled the stars to fight for the brave, and carved his way ahead with his sword, sweeping from his path whatever delayed his rise, and marching triumphant through the wreck he made.'

Lucan discarded the old epic device of making gods participate in human conflicts. Nevertheless his descriptions have the true epic quality, and Caesar's career gave him plenty of opportunities for splendid narrations. Caesar had spent many years in Gaul. Lucan gives a powerful description of a terrible place where the Celtic tribes of Gaul performed their human sacrifices. It is a dark wood where the sunlight cannot penetrate. Altars stand there, stained with dark rites of human sacrifice. No bird or beast will approach it. No wind ever stirs its leaves. If they rustle, it is with a strange, mysterious rustling all their own. There are dark pools and ancient trees, their trunks encircled by coiling snakes. Strange sounds and sights are there and even though the sun rides high at noon, even the priest will not approach the place for fear that he may come upon a terrible presence. Another episode in the life of Caesar which was given spirited narrative handling was his voyage to Italy in a fisherman's boat during a critical phase of his career. A storm overtakes the boat. 'It rocks helplessly in mid-sea. It sails in clouds, then dips its keel to the ground, for all the sea was piled into the waves and the heaped-up depths laid bare the sand.'

In spite of his immaturity, Lucan in this great poem had the understanding of historic developments to realise that both Pompey and Caesar were fighting for dictatorship. Therefore, he pays the highest tribute to Cato, the great statesman who had fought for the republican order all his life. Amidst the unabashed self-seeking and cruelty of the civil war, Cato stands as a shining figure. Inheritor of one of the richest legacies, Cato lived a simple life, untouched by the contamination of Roman luxury. He protected the state treasury from embezzlements by statesmen. He persuaded the Senate to issue an order that all candidates, soon after election, must come into court and give under oath a detailed account of their expenses. His implacable honesty left him not even a single friend in corrupt Rome. He fought every move, both by Caesar and Pompey, towards dictatorship. When Caesar at last overthrew the Republic, Cato died by his own hand, with a volume of philosophy by his side. Something of his idealism passed into Lucan and the young poet redeemed the many blemishes of his life in his penetrating intuition of what Rome lost in the battle which Caesar won. Even the yet unborn generations of Romans lost their right to live in freedom, in this battle, for the Caesar cult was to develop later into imperial absolutism. 'A deeper wound than their own age might bear was dealt to the peoples of the earth in this battle. It is more than life and safety that is lost. For all future ages of the world are we laid low. These swords have vanquished generations yet unborn and doomed them to eternal slavery.' Lucan realises that, in political life, the guilt or failure of one generation can be visited with punishment on a succeeding generation. 'What had the sons and grandsons of those who fought that day deserved that they should be born into slavery? Upon our necks is riveted the doom that we should live in fear of another.' Lucan feels the injustice of this and his conclusion clearly pointed to resistance: 'Fortune, since you gave a tyrant to those born since the war, you should have given them also a chance to fight for freedom.' Lucan fought against Nero and lost.

In Silius and Lucan, the epic retained something of the feeling for the understanding and creative reinterpretation of history which had made Virgil's epic one of the world's masterpieces. But in the rest of the epic tradition, this depth is lost and poets were content to limit themselves to a purely narrative excellence. Valerius Falccus, who also belongs to the first century of the Christian era, wrote an epic on the story of Jason and Medea. Jason was the Greek hero who went to a barbarian land to get its treasure, the Golden Fleece, and achieved his mission with the help of Medea, the daughter of the king of the land, who fell in love with him and betrayed her own father for her lover's sake. Apollonius of Rhodes had written a Greek epic on the theme. Though modelled on this work, the Latin work has its own individuality. Valerius has remarkable descriptive powers. He describes the wild coast of the barbarian land, dotted with sea caves, 'that never receive daylight's gifts nor the light of the heavenly orbs, homes of gloom all a-tremble with the sound of the deep.' He takes us to the underworld and builds up a weird landscape with his descriptions. 'Buried in the sunken silence of the eternal night lies that land. There the sun has never driven his flaming car, nor Jupiter sent forth his starry seasons. Silent are the leaves of its groves. There the ocean plunges roaring to its fall, there are plains desolate with dark fear. The shades go to and fro and after long silences, sudden voices thunder out.' The desolation, that follows in the silence after a band of women, sorrowing for their fallen men, had ceased their lamentations due to the sheer weariness of grief, is compared to the silence of Egypt when its birds have migrated to other lands—'as when the birds in mid-spring have returned to the north that is their home and their seasonal haunts on the banks of the sunny Nile are silent once more.'

This narrative power is adequate not only for the description of nature but also for vividly bringing out psychological states. There is a powerful description of the first night spent by Jason and his men in the strange land, so full of unknown threats:

'The dark hour deepened their fears when they saw the stars wheel slowly across heaven's vault and the peaks and fields of the earth disappeared from their view and all about them lay the horror of darkness. In the very stillness of things and the deep silence of the world, even the stars and the heaven, bejewelled with streaming trails of gold, affrighted them. And as one, benighted in a strange place amid paths unknown, pursues his fearful journey through the night and finds rest neither for eye nor ear, but only the blackness of the plain all around him and the trees that throng upon him, seen greater through the gloom, deepen his terror of the dark, even so the men trembled.'

Medea, the barbarian princess steeped in the superstitions of a primitive land and a devotee of terrible
gods, was of a dark, passionate nature and her love
for Jason was fated to bring him to a tragic despair
in the end, though immediately it benefited him in
his mission. This brooding, fateful quality of their
love is powerfully brought out in the description of
their first meeting. It is not the tenderness of love at
first sight that is depicted here, but the overwhelm-
ing emergence of passion, an explosion of dark
emotion, an explosion that will continue to wreak
havoc down the length of years. Medea is going for
midnight worship at the shrine of a terrible goddess.
She is alone in the silent night, chanting a song of
magic whereat all nature trembles. Jason comes
across her suddenly: 'as when in deepest night,
shades meet blind and voiceless in the deep of the
underworld, even so, in the darkness of the night
and of the grove, the two met, astonished, silent and
motionless like trees for one moment, before the
whirling breath of the storm wind has caught and
mingled their boughs.' Nevertheless, the poet treats
her with understanding. If she betrays her own
people for her lover, it is with an anguished heart.
'If your own valour can snatch you from the jaws of
death, even now, I pray you, let me be and send me
back guiltless to my father,' she pleads with Jason.
But he cannot succeed without her help and in the

dark hour before the dawn, when the tired stars had set, but dawn had not yet broken, she gave him the magical charms which would help him to conquer his obstacles and in surrendering them, it was as if 'she cast away her country and her own fair name and honour.' When at last, she and Jason flee from the land, Medea bids a pathetic farewell: 'O my father, would thou mightest give me now thy last embrace, as I fly to exile, and mightest behold my tears! Believe me, father, I love not him I follow more than thee. Would that the stormy deep might overwhelm us both! And may you find your children that remain more dutiful than me!' An old legend has been reborn with increased vitality in the epic of this poet.

Statius (AD 45–96), who was born in Naples, but spent his active life in Rome, was a very popular poet and was the favourite of the emperor Domitian. We shall study his lyrical poetry later. His most important work is the *Thebaid* or the Theban Story. It deals with the tragic story of Oedipus, whom a cruel fate made the murderer of his own father and the husband of his own mother, Jocasta, and of the civil war between his sons Polyneikes and Eteocles in which both were killed. Horror accumulates on horror, crime on crime, in this story. There is a moving description of Jocasta going on an unsuccessful mission to the battlefield to effect a reconciliation between her sons: 'Jocasta, her white hair streaming unkempt over her wild eyes, her cheeks all pale, her chest bruised by the beating of her anguished hands, came forth in all the majesty of the many sorrows.' The real hero of the poem seems to be Tydeus, the friend of Polyneikes who goes on a mission, like Krishna to the Kauravas, to plead with Eteocles for a share of the kingdom. The description of a scene in which he is ambushed by enemies is very vivid: 'Night began to shroud the sun with her humid pall and shed her blue darkness over the earth. He drew near the forest and from a high ground, saw the gleam of warriors' shields and plumed helmets, where the boughs of the wood left a space and, in the shadow before him, the quivering moonbeam played over their bronze armour. Astounded at what he saw, he yet pursued his way, though he unsheathed his sword. He was the first to speak. "Where are you from? And why do you hide thus, armoured for a fight?" There came no answer and their ominous silence told him that no peace or loyalty was there.' When Tydeus falls in the battlefield, he leaves the world without regrets or selfpity: 'I ask not that my bones be taken home. I care not for my last rites of funeral. I hate these limbs and this frail tenement, my body, that fails my spirit in my hour of need.'

Another heroic figure in the poem is a priest of the god Apollo who fights on the side of Polyneikes. The fates have decided that he should die in the field. Apollo, who loves him, becomes his charioteer like Krishna of Arjuna. But even the gods cannot save him. One thing, however, is granted to him: that he shall not fall in the field and lie like a neglected corpse denied a grave, but shall bodily pass on to the land of the dead. The hour comes. 'The earth gaped sheer and deep with vast abyss, and the stars of heaven and the shades of the land of the dead trembled with one accord. A vast chasm drew him down and swallowed his steeds as they made ready to leap the gulf. He loosed not the grip on rein or spur, but drove his chariot straight into Hades and, as he fell, gazed up for a last look at the heavens and the plains, till another shock once more united the gaping fields and shut out the light of the earth from Hades.'

The capacity of the poet for tenderness and moving pathos comes out in the portrayal of the character of Parthenopaeus, the son of Atalanta; who joined the war in spite of his very young age and in spite of the remonstrations of his mother. Like Abhimanyu, the young man stands out in all his glory among the more seasoned warriors. The imagery used here is very beautiful. 'When the stars are mirrored in tranquil, deep water and the reflection of the starry sky quivers in the waves, all the stars shine clear, but clearer than all does Hesperus send forth his rays; and as he gleams in the high heavens, even brighter do the blue waters show him forth.' The death of this young hero is one of the most moving passages in the epic:

'The boy fell into his comrades' arms and they bore him to a place apart. As he died, he wept for his fallen horse. His face dropped as they unbound his helmet, and a fading grace passed faintly over his quivering visage. The purple blood flowed from his breast of snow. At length he spoke these words through sobs that checked his utterance: "My life is falling from me. Go, my friends, comfort my unhappy mother. She indeed, if care and sorrow can give foreknowledge, has seen my woeful fate in dreams or through some omen. Yet do thou with loving art keep her terrors in suspense and long hold back the truth. Come not upon her suddenly, nor when she has a weapon in her hands; but when at last the truth must out, give her my message: 'Mother, I deserved my doom. I am punished, though my punishment breaks thy heart. I rushed to arms too young, and abode not at home when thou wouldst restrain me. Nor had I any pity for thine anguish in the day of battle. Live on then, and keep thine anger for my headstrong courage and fear no more for me. In vain thou gazest from the hills of our land, if any sound perchance may be borne from afar to thine ear through the clouds or thine eye have sight of the dust raised by our homeward march. I lie cold upon the bare earth, and thou art nowhere near to hold my head as my lips breathe farewell. Yet, childless mother take this lock of hair'"—and in his right hand he stretched it out to be cut away—"take this poor lock in place of my whole body, this lock of that hair which thou didst often comb. To it shalt thou give due burial and remember this also as my due. Let no man blunt my spears with unskilful use, nor any more drive the hounds I loved in hunts through any caverned glen. But this mine armour, whose first battle hath brought disaster, burn thou, or hang it to be a reproach to the gods' treachery".'

No epic poem of any literary merit was written after the first century and we may therefore turn to lyrical poetry.

3 Lyrical Poetry

Roman lyrical poetry begins with Catullus (84–54 BC) who is also one of the greatest poets in this tradition that Rome produced.

Catullus was born in Verona in north Italy, in a rich and influential family. His father had the privilege of being the host of Caesar whenever he came to Verona. Like other young men of talent from the outlying areas, he too was attracted by the brilliant life of the capital. At Rome he got into a company of young men who undoubtedly had talents and sensibility, but were tired of the austere Roman stoicism and were determined to sing of the sanctity of instinct, the innocence of desire and what logically followed, the heedless ecstasy of dissipation. Intense desire brings intense anguish in its wake and the greatness of Catullus lies in the fact that he could lay bare the ecstasy as well as the anguish of his spirit in flawless, sincere, musical verse.

Catullus fell in love with an aristocratic lady, Clodia. Her husband was away from Rome, as he was the governor of the province of Gaul, south of the Alps. Being of a very inconstant nature, she favoured the young poet in the beginning but soon turned to many other lovers. Catullus, to whom love was as intense an experience as it was to the Greek poet Sappho, wished to preserve this association in the poems he wrote to Clodia and therefore he addressed her as Lesbia, as Sappho had belonged to the island of Lesbos.

With youth's heedlessness of the conventions that are necessary for ordered social life, he asked Lesbia to ignore the criticism of the world, 'the grumbling of harsh old men', and continue to be his mistress. Youth, aflame with desire, felt all the more keenly the transience of things, and was passionately determined to burn out the brief hour of life in sheer ecstasy. 'Heaven's great lamps sink into the west; but they revive again in the east. But when once our brief sun has set, there comes the long sleep of everlasting night.' If at all he needed any justification for violating social conventions, the intensity and sincerity of his feeling were by themselves enough: 'No bond of plighted troth has ever been such as that true love wherewith I love you.'

The ardour which Lesbia awakened in him had too much intensity to be a joy. It was closer in spirit to pain, an abnormal, unhealthy excitement. We need not suspect any exaggeration when the young man wrote: 'My tongue is palsied. Rills of fire run through my veins. My ears listen fascinated to the throbbing of my heart. Mists veil my eyes.' The woman, much more mature in love affairs, used to allure him with subtle, indirect, erotic suggestions as is clear from the young man's poem to her pet sparrow: 'Sparrow, darling of my beloved, who plays with you and holds you to her breast, gives you her finger to peck and tempts you to bite sharply. I know not what dear jest it pleases my shining one to make of my desire!' But the bird died and his lament over it is moving. Perhaps he saw in it the symbol of the death of his own ecstasy. 'He was as sweet as honey and, hopping here and there; chirped continuously to his mistress only. Now he goes along the dark road to the place whence none returns.'

Lesbia soon wearied of him and turned to many new lovers. The raw, wounded humanity of the poet and his extreme youth made him strike at her and her lovers with blind fury. He taunts one of his rivals about his rheumatism and pictures the scene in bed when the gouty lover is unable to satisfy the aroused woman: 'Thus I am revenged each time they meet in bed. She is pale with nausea and with gout he is dead.' To another rival he declares: 'Embalmed in my verses, you shall stink through eternity.' As for Lesbia, he describes her as embracing three hundred lovers at once and in his anger he condemns the whole race of woman: 'A woman's words to her lover should be inscribed on the flowing winds, engraved upon swift streams.'

Such attacks should be blamed on the poet's extreme youth. The more valuable insights emerge from the clarity with which he analysed his own emotions when his dreams were all shattered. 'I loved you then, not as any man loves his mistress, but as a father loves his child. Now I know you. And though I burn with a stronger flame, yet you are far less precious and of less account. "How can that be?", you ask. Because such injury makes a man love with more desire and less affection.' The young man who had believed that desire was its own justification now received the greater gift that frustrated desire can give: an insight into one's own nature. He knew that it was the flaming intensity of one's own instinctual urges that shed a radiance on the loved object. But being a man, and especially a youth, this insight did not relieve him of his suffering. 'From now, I cannot feel affection for you if you become perfect, nor cease to desire you whatever you did...I hate and love. You ask how that can be. Who knows? I feel its truth and agony.'

Catullus made a great effort to build up again his shattered life. 'It is hard to cast accustomed love aside. It is hard, but there is a way if there is a will.' He chided himself: 'Wretched Catullus, play the fool no more. The lost is lost, dead love forever dead.' But in trying to forget, he remembers yet more vividly the old days. 'White were the suns that gleamed for you when your footsteps roamed where your beloved led.' The recollection grows in strength and reawakens the anguish with an immediacy of impact: 'Who now will be your lover? To whom shall you belong? Whom will you kiss? And bite whose lips?' When the meditation which began feeling its way towards self-control thus explodes with the charge of unspent emotion, the young man once again brakes its impetus and concludes with the admonition: 'But you, Catullus, remember to be strong!'

Though Catullus was rich, his way of living in the gay capital had built up a mountain of debts and since his love too was dead, he decided to seek a career in some overseas province of Rome. On the eve of his departure, he wrote his last farewell poem to Lesbia. He shows that though his wound might never heal, he was no longer a slave to his passion. 'Friends, while your comrade goes to seek his fortune where the Nile with her water colours the sea or where the rolling surf beats and again beats on the shores of some strange land, take this message to my beloved, a message brief, but not sweet. Bid her farewell for me. Let her keep the legion of her paramours, whose hearts she is bound to break like she broke mine. Let her not think at all of my love which, by her cruelty, met its death like a flower at the field's edge torn to shreds by a passing plough.'

Catullus got a job on the staff of the governor of Bithynia, the land that lay on the Black Sea coast of Asia Minor. Here the young man, who had so far lived in the currents and eddies of urban life, came into touch with profounder experiences. Once he had believed that life completely ended with death 'the sleep of an eternal night'. In this new region he came across the worship of the goddess Cybele and wrote a long poem which attests to his insight into the psychology of the religious temperament. Nevertheless, he was not happy in Bithynia and the homesick man at last decided to bid farewell to the land: 'Warm spring is here. The cold is gone. Raging winter has fled before spring's gentle breeze. It is on days like these that I long to leave this land and breathe the cleaner air of my home. "O for the road, the open way", I hear a voice within me cry. My eager feet brook no delay. Good bye, dear friends, good bye.' On his way home, he halted at a place near the ancient site of Troy, where his brother lay buried. His poem written on this occasion is very tender and moving: 'Over many a land, over many waters led, brother, my way to your grave is made. I have come to give you my salutations, to address the dust that cannot render one answering word. O thou by fate cut down, dear ghost, departed in thy first spring, accept your brother's offerings, wet with his tears, and his slow-spoken word. Greetings, brother, and, for evermore, farewell!'

Sailing through the Aegean and the Adriatic sea, he at last reached his estate on the island of Sirmio on Lake Garda. The homesick man greeted the island in an outburst of joy:

'Green-bright jewel, the gem of all the isles which the god of waters upholds in glassy lakes or the sea's expanse, it is good to look upon you. Even now I can scarcely think myself secure when I recall Bithynia's plains and see you near. After many months of travel, what happier way is there to escape the cares of the world than to return to our own home? Sleep is heaven, in our own beloved bed. Here is enough reward for exile and weary roads through foreign lands. Now my Sirmio, greet your master and make these waves bring laughter up, till the lake re-echo all the laughter in my home.'

Freed from his tormenting entanglement, his poetry became gentle, sensitive and exquisitely musical. His eyes, so long obsessed by the charms of Lesbia, learned to look on nature and found her even more beautiful than his mistress. Here is a description of a mountain stream that brought water to the grateful peasants: 'Upon a mountain crest, a crystal clear runlet leaps from the mossy boulders and takes no rest till it speeds down the valleys. The sun has cracked the fields and its cool stream seems a heaven-sent gift to toil-worn men.' His financial difficulties remained, but he learned to laugh at them. In a small poem to a friend, he describes how peaceful is his home, sheltered from both the north and south winds, but he adds that he knows no escape from the storm that is brewing over the mortgage on his house. In another poem, he invites another friend to come and stay with him, but warns that his purse is full of cobwebs and suggests that the friend himself bring wine and the provisions for food. The only thing he can give his friend is a bottle of attar of roses left over from his days in the fashionable capital, but he promises that the friend will find it of such fine quality that he will wish that he were made all nose. It is also likely that he at last understood the comradeship of marriage and the security and stability of the home, which were profounder realities than the heady excitement that comes from making a mistress of another man's wife and sharing her with many others. For, though he never married, he wrote a lovely wedding song on the occasion of the marriage of a friend of his. The song is supposed to be sung alternately by groups of youths and maidens. The maidens sing that a young girl is like a flower growing in a walled garden, caressed by the winds, strengthened by the soil, fostered by the dew. She is lovely and desirable while still intact but unloved as soon as she is wedded. The youths reply, 'The lonely vine which grows in a bare field never lifts itself up, never bears a sweet grape. But when it is wedded to the elm, the husbandsman tends it. So a maiden grows old untended. But when she becomes a wife, she is beloved by all, dear not only to her husband, but also to her community.' The song concludes with advice to the bride.

Catullus set the pattern for subsequent lyrical poetry. If he had been granted two decades more of life, instead of dying at thirty, his poetry might have evolved in the direction of a closer relation with life. That was not to be. And therefore the lyrical tradition that came to be established was impatient of social values and responsibilities, being often self-centred, though not necessarily selfish. It always started with the primacy of individual experience within a limited range of preoccupations and only when it suffered frustrations, did it go on to discover social values. The greatness of Virgil lies in the fact that he did not conform to this pattern laid by a poet who was fourteen years older than he. Nevertheless, he too could relax from his epic mood and involvement with the meaning of historical destiny and sing songs as limpid as any of the purely lyrical poets. To emphasise this aspect of Virgil's genius, which is apt to be overlooked, we need recall only one lyrical poem of his. It is supposed to be sung by a tavern maid inviting wayfarers into the inn:

'It is hot and dusty. Stay, travellers, abide here and drink a cup till all the world goes round. Here is a trellis-arbour cool with its shade of creepers and in our garden we have some one to play sweet music all day long on a shepherd's flute as they do in the fields. Our busy stream will gurgle softly near you, the while you drink and dream. We have made garlands for you, garlands of glorious, crimson roses or of white lilies that this morning were mirrored in their pool.

'You be damned, you there with the puritan eyebrows. You will need flowers only for laying on your tombstone. It is good to lie here under the vines. Tomorrow's care begone! Here is death twitching my ear. "Live now" says he, "for I am coming soon".'

Tibullus (54–18 BC), who was born in the year
Catullus died, repeats the pattern of life of the older
poet with only minor variations. His lands were
ruined when the civil war reached his region and
he drifted to Rome and fell in love with a woman
whom he addressed in his poems as Delia. We do
not know the identity of this lady. But, like the
Lesbia of Catullus, she too was a married woman.
The Roman general Messala gave Tibullus a job as
his aide-de-camp and took him to the eastern territories of Rome. When he returned to Rome he
found that his Delia had already found solace in the
arms of other lovers. While Catullus reacted by
striking out wildly against his rivals and his mistress,
Tibullus, who was of a more subdued temperament,
retired into melancholy brooding. It is probable that
he might have really wished to marry Delia after she
divorced her husband. For he recollects the dreams
he had of setting up a household with Delia who
would guard his corn and grapes and give warm
welcome to his friends. Such dreams have been
blown away with the wandering winds. Since his
sojourn in the capital has not been lucky, he turns
to the peace of the countryside. In his days of
happiness, he had known no law except youth's
sovereign right to live in the present: 'While the fates
allow, let us join our lives. Death will soon come,
with her head veiled in shadows. Heavy age will

soon creep up, and it will not be seemly to love, nor to say sweet things, with a white head.' But now he grew to a realisation of the sober strength of a life of work and relaxation in the open country, far away from the heady amusements of the city, with their bitter consequences.

He was content to contemplate a life of work in the fields, to rest under a tree, when the summer sun was riding high and watch the murmuring rivulet glide away, to rear swelling apples and nurse the vine tendril. Though he did not marry, he daydreamed about the quiet happiness of settled married life. 'How sweet to hear, outside, the howling blast of the rain-storm and strain a yielding mistress to my breast! Or, when the gusty torrent's rush has passed, to sink, lulled by beating rains, to sheltered rest!' It is likely that his thoughts also turned, like Virgil's, though with less intensity and depth, to the Golden Age 'when there were no armies, no hatred, and no war.' And he states his final creed: 'The hero is he whom, when his children have been begotten, old age overtakes in his humble cottage. He follows his herd, his son plays with the young of the herd, while the good wife heats the water for his weary limbs. So let me live till the white hairs glisten on my head, and I tell in my old man's fashion of the days gone by.'

Propertius (50–15 BC) sang of Cynthia as Tibullus sang of Delia and Catullus of Lesbia. The pattern is again the same. A young man from Umbria gets drawn into the whirlpools of the fashionable society of the capital, spends days of dissipation on the banks of the river Tiber, drinking wine in golden cups made by master craftsmen and watching the boats gliding by, falls headlong in love with a far more experienced society woman and is later rejected by her in favour of other lovers. The lover wants to bid her final farewell when his anger is at its white heat, for he knows that once it cools the bondage will still remain. He threatens to immortalise her disloyalty in his poetry and warns her that if she preferred younger men to him, time is pursuing her also relentlessly and soon her mirror shall reveal wrinkles appearing one by one on her face.

It is when he has released himself wholly from the bondage that his poetry flows out of this stagnant triviality. When his friend Paulus lost his young wife Cornelia, Propertius wrote a beautiful poem in which he is moved by the holiness of wedlock which he could not realise in his younger days. The shade of Cornelia is imagined as appearing before her husband and addressing him:

'Cease, beloved, to assail my tomb with tears. When the ferryman of the river of the dead has taken his fare, the great door closes on the spirits of the departed and the grass grows on their tombs. The dark doors open to no prayer. The streams of your tears shall run to waste on these desert shores.

'I am now a burden that five fingers could lift. Nights of my doom, and you, slow shallows of the marshes, and waves coiling about my feet in the land of the dead, I came here before my time, but not in guilt. The gods of our hearth have blushed for no shame of mine. Nature gave me laws, inherited with my blood, so that I did not need the fear of punishment to lead a life of virtue.

'Now I commend to you our common pledges, our children. Even in my ashes, anxiety for them lives unburnt. Bereaved father of the household, be also a mother now to them!'

In his later years Propertius realised that everything is doomed to decay, while human worth alone can abide in this general ruin, at least in the memory of subsequent generations: 'Neither the pyramids raised high to reach the stars, nor even the heaven of Jupiter, nor all the wealth lavished on the tombs of the great, can escape the final law of death. Either their glory is sapped by fire or rain, or they fall beneath the blows of the years, crushed by their weight. But the name which genius seeks does not vanish from time. The glory of genius abides without death.' His last message was that human ambition and agitation were futile fretfulness and that the only thing that counted was the life of the mind.

And now we come to a poet who, though he belongs to the same group, was of a much greater stature than Tibullus and Propertius. Ovid (43BC to AD17) was born at Sulmo, in a pleasant valley of the Apennine range, about ninety miles from Rome. He came from a rich middle class family and his father sent him to Rome intending to train him for a public career. After beginning an official career which would have ultimately made him a senator, Ovid suddenly gave it up and decided to devote himself to poetry, in spite of the warning of his father that a literary career was the straight way to death by hunger.

Ovid's lighthearted temperament refused to be impressed by Virgil's *Aeneid*. He claimed that since Rome had been founded by the son of Venus, the goddess of love, the duty of the Roman citizen was to dedicate himself to the arts of love. He fell in love with a woman whom he addressed in his poems as Corinna. He wrote poems to her instructing her how to communicate with him by means of signs even when she was in the company of her husband. He quarrelled with her and got reconciled again, but noticed that her mastery of the arts of love had increased greatly during their estrangement; obviously she had the benefit of many other tutors. Therefore, he decided that constancy was a handicap and decided to make love to every pretty woman in Rome. In his first volume, a collection of love poems, he declared this creed: 'It is no fixed beauty that calls my passion forth. There are a hundred causes to keep me always in love. If it is some fair one with modest eyes downcast, I am aflame and her innocence is my temptation. If it is some saucy jade, I am smitten because she is well versed in the arts of love. If she is austere, I judge she would yield, but is deep in her conceit…My love is the candidate for the favours of them all.' He is afraid that his simultaneous duties to so many mistresses will undo him, but he will be happy to die like an exhausted soldier on the field of love.

With the heady obstinacy of youth, Ovid dismissed all criticism and declared that he was content to be called 'the well-known singer of his own worthless ways.' He loved Rome because there were more pretty wenches in this city than there were fish in the sea or leaves in the woods or stars in the sky. There was great truth in his assumption that the city had become the great capital of Venus, for Rome's fashionable society spent most of its time in flirting with each other's wives. Ovid claimed that the Roman women of the olden days might have been content to attend to their domestic duties and bring up their children, but the modern girls were of a quite different temperament, loving finery and flirtation, and he was writing for them. Therefore, in his next work, *Art of Love*, he declared that he had been appointed by Venus as tutor of the ways of love and went on to give lessons in the art of seduction. He also wrote a poetic manual on cosmetics telling young girls how to improve their beauty by using various preparations.

His next work was less frivolous. Entitled *Heroines*, it retold the love stories of famous women in myth and legend, each poem being in the form of a letter written by the woman to her lover. Several of the stories were of a tragic nature and their treatment is tender and moving. Thus Oenone, the nymph whom Paris deserted for Helen, recalls the days of their happiness when they had roamed the woodlands together, sleeping under trees on summer nights, sheltering in humble cottages during snow and rain. Paris, in the tenderness of adolescent love, had carved his beloved's name on many young trees in the forests: 'The trees you carved still keep their clear marking and all can read my name graven there. As the trunks grow, so grows my inscribed name. Let these trees grow, for they will yield you plenty of wood for my funeral.' Penelope writes to Ulysses separated from her in the long drawn out Trojan war. She chides him for his long absence which has made her a widow though her husband is alive. She narrates with a touch of humour how the returned soldiers haunt taverns and, wetting their fingers with drops of wine, draw the Trojan battle field on the tables and weary their listeners with their own versions of the progress of the campaign. She recounts with feeling the joys of reunion of the other women whose men had returned, and her own anxieties. She concludes at last: 'This letter your Penelope sends you, dallying Ulysses. Write no reply, but come yourself.' Perhaps the most moving poem in this collection is the lament of Ariadne who had helped the Athenian prince, Theseus, to slay a fierce monster but was deserted by him on a lonely island when she was sleeping by his side:

'It was the hour when the earth is first spread with night dew and the birds hidden in the leafage raise their plaint. Half-waking, still languid with sleep, I put out my hands as I lay, to touch Theseus. There was no one. I tried again, but on that couch no one was by my side. Fear shook off sleep. I rose in terror and flung myself from the widowed bed. The moon still shone. I gazed along the shore and saw the sand—but sand and nothing more. I ran hither and thither in dismay. I called out his name, but only echoes from the cliff-side responded.'

Ovid's next attempt was a very ambitious one. He wrote a long narrative beginning with the mythology about the creation of the world and coming down to contemporary history. The first eight sections dealt with the gods of Olympus. The next section dealt with Hercules, the demigod, a hero born of a divine father and a mortal mother. The next two sections narrated the stories of such legendary figures as Orpheus and Adonis. The Trojan war where mythology draws nearer to history took up the next two sections. In the next section we come with Aeneas to Italy and the fifteenth section concludes with the reception of Julius Caesar into heaven. Ovid, however, lacked the sustained narrative power needed for an epic and the work really becomes a vast collection of two hundred and fifty stories—a great performance. The book was titled *Metamorphoses* because every story involved some supernatural transformation, as when the nymph Daphne, pursued by Apollo, changed into a laurel and Halcyone, mourning for her drowned husband, turned into a sea bird. The narrative gives him plenty of opportunities to use local legends. Thus, Poseidon, the god of the sea, describes how he was enraged when a group of nymphs offered worship to all the other gods but forgot him. He raised the sea to a vast height, the raging torrent of waters swallowed up the land and the forested hills inhabited by the nymphs became islands in the sea. Another story deals with the peasant couple, Baucis and her husband Philemon. The gods visited their village in disguise and were refused hospitality by everyone except this couple. For their generosity, the gods grant them a boon. Their only request is that they should live and die together, so that the old man with his withered arms will not have to carry his wife to the funeral pyre and the woman will be spared the anguish of shedding a widow's tears over her husband. The boon is granted and when the hour comes, the couple is transformed into two young trees, with their branches interlaced.

Ovid had just completed this volume when a blow fell with the speed of lightning. Augustus issued an order banishing him from Rome to Tomi on the Black Sea, a cold, inhospitable town which is called Constanta today. We do not have the complete background to this. But it is clear that the whole frivolous poetic tradition from Catullus to Ovid must have proved a great irritant to the statesman who was doing everything in his power to effect a moral regeneration of the nation. Only hard work could build up the nation. But Phaedra, one of Ovid's heroines, who fell in love with her stepson, declared that virtue was whatever brought pleasure; the poet was determined to sing about his own 'worthless ways' and the impressionable mind of Roman youth was being nourished on metrical lessons on seduction. Rome needed soldiers to consolidate the realm, while Ovid sang that the lover was a greater hero than the soldier because he risked rain and snow and darkness in going to his midnight assignments. While teaching the art of love, Ovid had also given lessons in curing love. 'It is useful to surprise your lady in the morning, before she has completed her toilet. The best remedy is hard work, next hunting, third absence.' But Ovid himself showed no inclination to do any hard work and the Roman youth who read him had only one ambition —to fall exhausted in the field of love, weary with too many conquests. Augustus's irritation exploded when he found that the corruption of morals invaded his own household. His granddaughter Julia, a married woman, had outraged even the tolerant Roman society by her scandalous looseness of conduct. Ovid belonged to her circle. Augustus banished her also when he took against the poet.

The controversy between the autonomy of art, its alleged privileges transcending morality and the counterclaim of the paramount demands of social order and health is an ancient one and therefore, in this context, we give without comment Ovid's defence of himself, leaving it to the reader to judge its merits:

'My *Art of Love* is not a serious work. But it contains nothing contrary to the laws. Besides, it is not addressed to Roman ladies. It is a light work for light women. "Oh, but a respectable married woman can practise an art intended for others," some may say. Then she must read nothing. For, from every poem she can learn something towards sinning. If she is bent on vice, every book she takes up will form her character for it. This does not mean that every book is criminal. There is no good thing which cannot also do harm. And where should one stop? If poetry corrupts, plays also offer the seeds of vice. Have all the theatres put down, which have given so many cause for sinning! Put down the theatre; there the young girl sits next to a complete stranger! Why is that portico left open? Some women walk there to meet their lovers! And an honest woman should avoid the temples. In the Temple of Jupiter she will at once think how many women the god made mothers. At the Temple of Mars the statue of Venus stands before the door, together with that of her husband whom she repeatedly betrayed.

Even Aeneas was her son through her irregular association with Anchises. Everything can corrupt perverse minds.'

Even those who believe that Ovid was perfectly justified in finding his life's mission, if he thought fit, in writing light works for light women, must recognise the deeper poetic qualities of his work after tragedy came into his life. On the voyage of exile he began a volume of poems entitled *Sorrows*. His poem on the scene of farewell is very moving. Fearful of offending Augustus, many of his former friends absented themselves at the time of his departure. His wife was there, overcome with grief, and she remained loyal to his memory throughout. A brooding sorrow prevailed over the scene as if it was a funeral. On the way, a tempest arises and Ovid describes it vividly. In his tormented mood, the billows seemed to rise to the stars while the hollows between the waves sank to the depths of hell. Above, the storm clouds rioted fiercely; below, the desert waste of waters was seized by one vast convulsion. He wished that the storm would bury his ship in the deep so that all his misery would end.

At last he reached Constanta and his next volume, *Letters from the Black Sea*, contains poems which the homesick man addressed to friends at home, describing his life of exile. The bleak landscape of the region chilled his sensitive spirit. It was a bare, rocky stretch of land where nothing would grow. The sun seemed for ever shut out by the mists that rolled in from the Black Sea. It seemed to be a land of perennial winter: 'The snow lies deep. The sun is too weak to melt it away and the snow stays in drifts unmelted all the year. The tempestuous north wind blows fiercely all the year long, levelling towers of stone and carrying roofs away. Men go about completely wrapped up in woollen cloth and you can see only their eyes. Water is brittle here. You have to use a spade. Running streams are made solid by the frost. Even the dark blue surface of the river Danube has congealed into ice. We go on foot across the river. Horse's hoofs ring loud where once the boatmen plied their oars.'

Memories of blue Italian skies tormented him. He recalled his own native place, the valley of Sulmo with its vineyards, olive groves, corn fields and running streams. He envied his poems which could go to Italy: 'Go, my book, and in my name, greet the dear earth of my native land!' A new, poignant note had entered his poetry. He wondered whether even time could mellow his sorrow: 'Time swells the clusters till each grape can scarcely contain the juice. Time mellows fruits and from the seed brings forth the white shoot. It wears away the ploughshare's tooth. It breaks the flint, the steel. It gives relief to stricken hearts. It calms the wrath men feel. All things must yield to slowly moving age. Only my sorrows will never be assuaged by time.'

Ovid was fifty-one when he was sent into exile. For a long time he hoped that a pardon would come and he would be able to go back. It never came and he died in exile after nine weary years. His death, or rather his exile, marked the end of a tradition—that of a sophisticated poetry, urban in background and feeling, brilliant and polished always, but often lacking in depth and always in range. Subsequent poetry left the drawing room for the open country and if it sang of love it was with the poignant notes of the poems which Ovid wrote in the days of his loneliness.

A long narrative poem on the volcano Aetna has come down to us from an anonymous writer who wrote between the death of Ovid in AD 17 and AD 70. The theme enabled the writer to display his narrative powers in the description of an awe-inspiring natural phenomenon: 'Suddenly Aetna burst its caves and, glowing with fire, cast forth all that its furnaces contained. A vast wave, swift and hot with fire, streamed forth afar. Crops blazed along the fields, forest and hill glowed rosy red.' The writer weaves a human story into this sequence. While men and women flee from the liquid fire, groaning under the weight of their possessions, two brothers ignore all their wealth and their own safety and carry their old parents on their backs and fight through the crowds to safety. 'The fire feeds on all it meets; nothing will it spare, or, if aught it spares, only the pious.' The flames do not touch the devoted sons. A Virgilian emphasis on the sacredness of filial duty has been used to give human interest to a poem on nature and in spite of the rhetoric with which the moral of the poem is emphasised, it has the thrill of spirited narration, sustained with dramatic suspense.

Yet another echo from Virgil is found in the work of another writer of the first century, Columella. He came from Spain but took up agriculture in Italy. He made a study of the problems of agriculture and wrote a classic on the subject which was published in AD 65. He was sorry to note that the best agricultural lands were kept out of production by the rich, who used them for their stately country residences. The next best lands were taken up by olive groves and vineyards. Only inferior soils were left for growing corn. 'We have abandoned the care of our soil to our lowest slaves and they treat it like barbarians.' The free men of Italy, he felt, were degenerating in cities when they should have been hardening themselves by working the earth. 'We spend our time in theatres and circus grounds rather than among crops and vines.' He loved the soil and felt that the life of work under the rural skies led to a profounder culture of the spirit than the bookish culture of the towns. Farming, he said, was 'a blood relative of wisdom.' His whole outlook had close affinities with that of Virgil in his poem on agriculture. He loved gardening too and his seasonal cycle was punctuated by the rhythm of the growth of not only the food crops but also of flowers, valuable only because of their beauty.

Columella personified the earth freely in his poetry. When the season for sowing comes, sweet earth should be adorned anew, her old raiment of green weeds must be stripped from her by the plough, her throat quenched by irrigation, her hunger satisfied by fertilising manure. 'Now cool spring has come, the gentlest season of the year, when the sun is young and not too warm and bids us recline in the young herbage. It is sweet to drink the rill that flows among the murmuring grass, with waters neither icy cold nor warm with the sun's heat.' The spring is also dear because it is the season when the garden is resplendent with the colours of the rainbow, the blushing red of the rose, the gold of the sunflowers and the blue of the lotus.

Another contemporary poet who adopted pastoral themes was Calpurnius. He wrote about the life of the herdsman in the same lyrical vein as Columella wrote about the tiller of the soil. 'When spring is young and the birds begin to pipe once more, and the swallow returns to build its nest anew, then move all your flock from its winter fold. For then the wood sprouts in fresh glory with its spring shoots and builds anew the shades of summer with the thick fresh foliage of trees. Then all the glades are bright with flowers and the green year is born again.' He loved the rural deities and put up their wooden images among his 'vine-clad elm trees, where the jewelled stream rolls its green waves and with rippling water runs through the lilies.'

With Petronius we return to the highest stratum of Rome's fashionable society, but the marvel is that from the beginning there was a deep core of strength in the man which held fast without being wholly drowned in the eddies of dissipation, though this was not apparent to the casual observer. He is one of the most unforgettable figures in Rome's literary annals. According to tradition he came from Marseilles and even at the height of his dissipation he was distinguished by a refined elegance and good taste which are the qualities of the French temperament at its best. Nero, who was very sensual but also very crude, made him the arbiter of elegance and Petronius gradually found himself the master of revels at the emperor's court. For some time, he held office as the governor of Bithynia and surprised everybody by his energetic and capable administration. But back in Rome, he found that the company of Nero was incompatible with serious work and he became indolent, passing his days in sleep and his nights in revelry. Tacitus, the historian, said of him that he idled into fame. His companions found that they could not regard him as a rake like themselves, for though he indulged his appetites in their company, he did so with an air of luxurious ease, of refinement and judgment. He was an educated and elegant voluptuary. But the friendship of Nero proved dangerous as it had proved in the case of Lucan. Perhaps the crude emperor secretly envied his air of distinction. When Nero was putting down a conspiracy against himself, a rival of Petronius falsely testified against him and Petronius died as he lived, in a leisurely, carefree manner. He opened his veins and while life was ebbing away, he conversed with his friends—not on the gravest of themes, nor in the key of the dying hero. He listened to no disquisitions on the immortality of the soul or the dogmas of philosophy, but discussed playful verses. The casual manner of his death masked a courage, just as the casual manner of his life concealed the deeper levels of his personality. Two years later, in AD 68, Nero too was dead.

Petronius has also written some charming trifles. Thus, when a lady playfully pelts him with a snow ball, he marvels that this missile of ice can light a fire in him and he requests her to quench the fire, not with more snow, but with an equal fire. But the bulk of his poetry belongs to a higher level of intensity. Perhaps, as in the case of the French poet Baudelaire, a high sensual excitability was an inherited trait in his nature. One of his poems reveals the irresistible strength of this stormy blood. 'I had just gone to bed and begun to enjoy the first stillness of the night and sleep was slowly overcoming my eyes, when suddenly awakened passion jerked me up by the hair and said, "you are my slave, the lover of a thousand girls. How can you lie thus alone?" I leapt from my couch, and barefoot, with dishevelled robe, started on my errand, yet never accomplished it. Now I hurry forward, now I am loth to go. At last I am ashamed to stand thus aimless in mid-street. There is no sound of voices, the roar of the streets is hushed, not a bird twitters, no watch dog barks. And I, alone of all men, dread to return to my bed, and wander, ruled by a mighty lust.'

A settled marital life was difficult for him, with this highly excitable temperament. He defended himself wittily. 'People say that one should love one's wife, as one loves one's fortune. But I do not desire to love always even my fortune.' Nevertheless, he learned to distinguish between the stormy experience of lust and the more elevated experience and enduring strength of love. 'Delight of lust is gross and brief and weariness follows in the wake of desire. We are not beasts and love sickens in lust and the fire dies. But in eternal holiday, beloved, let us lie still and kiss the hours away. No weariness is here, nor repentant shame, but a lasting happiness. Never can this ecstasy end, but it is ever an ever-renewed beginning.' He realised that lust was a union of bodies while love could be a meeting of souls in rapture. 'Ah God, ah God, that night when we two clung so close, our hungry lips transfused our souls and death met its death!' He had also an intuition that such love could grow in strength and not diminish as the years went by, taking away with them the beauty of youth, which often stimulated only physical passion. 'Beloved, let that night be for ever dear, the night that laid you first upon my heart. Let all those memories be dear, the bed, the quietly burning lamp and your tenderness. Let us continue to love, although the years be hasting and soon time shall be erased for us. Old love should last. Oh, God, do thou prevent that what was swift begun were swift to end.'

Deep within him, this man, who participated in the dissipations of Rome's highest social circles, loved peace and quiet. He loved the sea, but not as a symbol of challenge to man:

'Let Ulysses go sail the stormy waters. The contented man should know only this much of the sea's power. He should venture only where the tide flows back and the wave bathes his feet without peril, where the mussel is thrown up among the green sea-weed, where the curled shells are gently rolled along by the wavelets. Where the wave turns the sands to rush back in the eddy, there pebbles of many a hue are revealed on the wave-washed floor of gleaming sand.'

When revisiting regions by the sea where his boyhood had been spent, the ancient rock pools where the sea weed swayed evoked precious memories and he murmured to himself, 'Here is the harbour for a stilled desire.' It is not that he lacked courage or a spirit of adventure. But the sea symbolised for him the perils and frustrations that follow in the wake of a life of ambition, a life exhausted in the pursuit of transient values. The lives of the mariner and the shepherd became for him contrasted symbols of ambition and content. 'There sea and sky struggle and buffet each other. Here the tiny stream runs through smooth and smiling country. There the sailor laments for his sunken ship, here the shepherd takes his flock to the gentle river. There death confronts greed, here the smiling fields bow before the curved sickle.'

He had a small house in the countryside to which he used to escape often from the dissipations of the capital. 'My cottage is small, but it is quiet under its roof. An elm tree shelters it under its shade and the vine climbs up the tree with the grape bursting with sweet juice. The fruit trees look as if they will break beneath the rich burden of their branches. Where the garden bed's light soil drinks in the runnels of water, flowers grow in profusion.' Of all the seasons, he loved autumn especially, for the earth then fulfilled her promise of ripened corn and fruit. 'Now autumn has brought its cool shades and the sun's rays are less hot as he has started voyaging towards winter. The trees have begun to shed their leaves. No more young shoots appear on the vine, which is nursing to ripeness its last clusters of grapes. Before our eyes is spread all the promise of the year.' He might again be drawn back into the eddies of the life at the court, but he knew that he could find real peace only here. 'Go, then, and barter the hours of flying life for rich banquets,' he told himself, but added, 'But I pray that my destined end may find me here and here demand an account of how I have spent my vanished hours.'

Some of these poems have a burden of thought but carry it easily. In one poem he studies the origin of dreams and sees them as the fulfilment in fantasy of the wishes that reality frustrated. 'The body lies quiet in sleep and the mind, set free, follows in darkness what it sought by day. The sailor rescues from the sea his ship, or drowning, clings to it. The lass writes a love-letter to her lad and in his sleep the hound is hot upon the tracks of the hare.' As the wish created a world of fulfilment in dreams, fear created a similar world in myth and religion. 'It was fear that first created gods in the world, when the lightning fell from high heaven and the ramparts of the world were rent with flame and even mountain peaks were smitten and blazed. The sun became a god who sank to rest after he had traversed the sky since dawn. The moon goddess grew old and once more renewed her glory. Soon there were gods to claim the first share of the peasant's harvest of corn or the wine from the first crushing of grapes. The sea became the realm of the god Neptune who swam deep-plunged beneath all the waters of the world. The fantasy spread and the man who has betrayed the world for gold now strives greedily to create gods of his own.'

Petronius was drawn deeper into the dissipations of the capital's life than Propertius or Tibullus, but deep within him was his real self that maintained its poise amid all the unhealthy excitement. While they were punished only by frustrations he had to confront death. 'This is the proof of the noble character: that a man has shown no fear,' he had said. He redeemed his life and vindicated his real character by the causal manner in which he confronted his premature death.

Statius (AD 45–96), whose epic poem on the Theban legend we have already glanced at, has left a collection of lyrical poems also. This poet from Naples who became the favourite of the emperor Domitian, was distinguished by the limpid clarity of his verse. His lighter poems describe everyday events, festivals, holidays. One of them cherishes the memory of a palace by the sea belonging to a friend of his, where he had spent a pleasant holiday:

'One of the rooms looks to the east and receives the first light of the morning sun. Another keeps the sun company when he sets and receives the last gleam of expiring light, when the day is outworn and the shadow of the dark hill on which the castle stands falls athwart the deep and the great castle swims reflected in the glassy sea. These rooms are full of the sound of the ocean, while there are others that know not the roar of the waves, but cherish silence and quiet. Each room has a joy that is its own. Each has its own view of the sea and each window frames its own landscape of ocean and land.'

His poem to sleep on a restless night when he was tired has the same limpid music. 'By what crime or error, O sleep, most gentle of gods, have I, that am young, deserved that I alone should lack thy blessing? All cattle and birds and beasts of the wild lie silent. The curved mountain ridges seem as though they slept the sleep of weariness and wild torrents have hushed their roaring. The waves of the deep have subsided and the seas, reclined on earth's bosom, take their rest.'

His lyrical poetry could ascend to more poignant levels, as in the poem he wrote to a friend who had lost a young protegé of his:

'Come, soothe your anguish and light up your head that droops with sorrow. You see all things dead or soon to die. Day and night and stars all pass away, nor shall its massive frame save the world from destruction. As for the tribes of earth, this mortal race, and the death of the multitudes all doomed to pass away, why bewail them? All that has birth must bow before death. We all must go, must go.'

Several of the Roman emperors were interested in literature. Tiberius (42BC to AD37) was the type of scholar who wasted his energy in probing issues like who the mother of Hecuba was, or what the name of Achilles was when he was disguised as a girl by his mother who did not want him to go for the Trojan war. Caligula (AD 12–41) had the common sense approach to literary criticism and he described Seneca's oratory as 'sand without lime', an excellent summing up of the latter's lack of cohesiveness. Nero (AD 37–68) wrote lyrics and an epic on Troy. But he often managed to get the first prizes in poetic contests awarded to himself. He also had a high opinion of himself as an actor. When Nero was acting in a play, nobody was allowed to leave the hall, even for the most urgent of purposes and one historian states that there were several cases of women giving birth to babies in the middle of the performance. He played the role of Hercules and Orestes in Greek tragedies and this unbalanced man was touched by the madness of Hercules and was guilty of matricide like Orestes.

Hadrian (AD 76–138) was a great administrator who promised he would look after the empire, keeping always in mind that it was the people's property and not his own. Once, weary with work, he was forced to refuse audience to a woman with a petition with the plea that he had not the time. 'Don't be emperor then,' she cried. He immediately granted her a hearing. His final years were terribly unhappy. The boy this childless man had adopted as his son and probable successor drowned in the Nile and Hadrian, during his last days, was tormented by some acutely painful disease. He ordered his bodyguard to kill him, but he fled in horror. A similar order to his doctor made the poor man commit suicide. Hadrian left this lyric just before he died:

> *Soul of mine, little waif,*
> *Guest and partner of my clay,*
> *Now you will go off to a place*
> *So grey, so stark, so bare*
> *Never to play again, never to play.*

An anonymous poem has come to us from the third century. It sings of Venus, the goddess of love. This exquisite poem begins with a lyrical description of the advent of spring, recovers the ancient vision of love as the secret, creative energy of the world which leads it to all its fulfilments, and closes again on an intensely personal lyrical note. 'Spring is young, spring now is calling. Spring is the world reborn. In spring the beloved grants her favours to her lover, the birds mate and the woodland loosens her tresses under nuptial showers.' According to the ancient myth, Venus was full-born from the foam of the sea.

The poet imagines a spring shower whipping up the foam on the sea and the birth of Venus thus becomes the fruit of the union of the god of gods, Jupiter, who sent the rain and his bride, the earth. 'From the moisture overhead and the orbed seafoam, amid the multitudes of the green waves and the living things of the sea, sprang Venus, wave-born from the union of shower and spray.' The first showers that usher in the spring become renewed symbols of the marriage of earth and sky. 'To quicken the whole year from the clouds of spring, the bridegroom-shower has flowed into the lap of his fair bride, the earth, and coursing through the land in rivulets to the sea, the life-sustaining water again rises to the sky as rain-bearing clouds that nourish all the lands in the vast frame of the earth.' Born of the marriage of earth and sky, the goddess of love becomes the symbol of the creative energy of nature.

'She herself paints the crimsoning year with flowery jewels: herself coaxes swelling buds into warm clusters under the spring wind's breath; herself sprinkles the dripping wetness of the glittering dew that the night-air leaves as it passes. The sparkling dew-drops quiver in the wind, then stretch, ready to fall. The little dew-bead holds together in its fall. The moisture that the stars distil on cloudless nights unfolds the maiden buds from their wet sheaths at day-break.

The goddess loosens the green girdle of the rose-bud and the full-blown bloom blushes red, conscious of her maidenhood. The goddess floods with her energy the little seed and the vast processes that go on in the earth and sky nourish it and the goddess pours quickening life into the tender shoot, bidding the universe know the mysteries of birth. Herself, the creator in hidden might sways flesh and spirit from within with her enkindling life.'

So the limpid verse flows on, finding the secret spell of the great goddess of love in the fertilising rain, in the flowers of spring, in the songs of merry festivals, in the vague disquiet in the blood during adolescence, in timid trysts in woodland solitudes. And after each stanza comes the golden promise of the chorus. 'Tomorrow shall be love for the loveless, and for the lover tomorrow shall be fulfilment.' The conclusion transforms the universal exaltation into an intensely felt personal emotion. 'Now the graceful swans speed over the pools calling to their mates. Hid in the leafy shade the nightingale sings. She sings. I alone am silent. When will my spring come? When shall I be like the bird, that I may cease to be voiceless and break into song?'

By the fourth century, the lyrical genius of ancient Rome had exhausted itself. This century has only one poet of any merit—Claudian. He was born in the eastern region of the empire and Greek was his mother tongue. But he came to Italy, learned Latin and became the favourite of many high placed Romans including the emperor Honorius. He retold the story of Persephone or Proserpine as she was called by the Romans. This goddess was carried away by Pluto, the god of the dark nether world but was allowed to revisit the earth once every year. She is the symbol of spring and Claudian narrates the story with great tenderness and the poem is studded with haunting pictures of land and sea. He wrote a great poem in praise of Rome:

'Praise be to the mother city, who extends her sway on the earth and was the earliest cradle of justice. This is the city which, sprung from humble beginnings, has stretched to either pole and from one small place extended its power so as to be coterminous with the light of the sun. It is she alone who has received the conquered into her bosom, and like a mother, not an empress, protected the human race with a common name, summoning those whom she has defeated to share her citizenship, and drawing together distant races with bonds of affection. To her rule of peace we owe it that the world is our home. Thanks to her we are all one people.'

A lesser poet of the same century, Rutilius, also echoed these thoughts when he sang of Rome: 'Of the diverse nations you have made a single motherland.' But the tributes were more true of the past than of contemporary times and it was like singing of spring just before the explosion of a thunder storm. For Claudian died only in the beginning of the fifth century and the same century saw the end of ancient Rome under the impact of virile tribesmen.

4 Philosophy and Criticism in Poetry

If Roman poetry, especially of the sophisticated youth of the metropolis, was content to sing about society women with many lovers, we must not forget that it developed the range and depth to give a profound meaning to history in the works of Virgil. Philosophical thought and social criticism also permeated poetry and the marvel is that this did not lead to prosaic verse, but to genuine poetry where the thought is coloured with feeling and finds expression in a sustained music.

Ennius (239–169 BC) seems to have been the first poet in this tradition. In one of his poems, instead of using myths for poetic narration, he tries to offer a theory about myths. He inclined to a form of naturalism, interpreting the old religious myths of naturalistic ideas. Jupiter is simply the universe in a perpetual state of change, the air which becomes wind, and cloud, and rain, matter in its various forms nourishing all life. Later, he gave an alternative view according to which the gods were old heroes who lived in the first phases of the race's history and were subsequently deified by the imagination of men.

The greatest poet of the philosophical tradition in Roman literature is Lucretius (95–51 BC). We have very little biographical data about him. Probably he belonged to the aristocracy. Anyway, we have a clear idea of the period in which he lived and its anarchy, as a solution for which he wrote his great poem, *On the Nature of Things*. His period saw the climax of the class wars, the massacres perpetrated by adventurers like Marius and Sulla, the revolt and suppression of Catiline, the establishment of Caesar's dictatorship. The uprooting of social life had turned many into atheists and the majority of the masses into a mob steeped in superstition. From Asia Minor, the cult of a terrible goddess, who exacted animal and probably human sacrifices, spread to Rome. Astrology became widely believed and people would not embark on any venture without waiting for the propitious hour. The idea of a hell where people would be visited with incredible tortures gained ground. The sun and moon were conceived as gods and every eclipse struck the rural areas and the city slums with a superstitious terror. Those who were intelligent enough to be free from such superstitions turned out to be uninhibited self-seekers who tried to increase their wealth and power at the expense of others. Lucretius felt that, in such a crisis, only a fundamental rethinking about nature and man's place in her evolving scheme, could restore the certitude which could lift people from the quagmires of superstition and give them the urge and energy to reconstruct their shattered lives.

What most shocked the sensitive spirit of this great Roman was the foul crimes committed in the name of religion. 'To so many evils religion has persuaded men,' he declares. He recalls the legendary sacrifice of Iphigenia to appease the gods and the bloody, unclean sacrifices that were even then being perpetrated in the worship of the Phrygian mother goddess. He traces all these excesses to the blind terror inspired in the unthinking mind by the vast powers of nature, which seem hostile to man and before which man shrinks into utter insignificance. Lucretius fully understands the intensity of this feeling of insecurity.

'When we look upward at the great vault of heaven and the empyrean fixed above the shining stars, and consider the paths of sun and moon, then in our breasts, burdened with other ills, this dread will also start into life. We are compelled to the belief that it is the immeasurable might of unseen gods, dreaded beings, that moves the blazing stars along their diverse ways...And then what man is there whose heart does not shrink with terror of these unseen beings, whose limbs do not creep with fear, when the parched earth trembles at the lightning stroke and the roar of thunder rolls through the sky!'

In order to understand the moral courage behind the attempt made by Lucretius to restore order in the prevailing anarchy by resolutely applying reason, we must bring out the hidden significance of this passage.

Primitive religion arose out of fear, when the imagination of man peopled storm and flood, lightning and thunder with personified, but unseen, powers and primitive ritual was a means to appease these powers. Roman society had evolved very much ahead of this primitive mentality. But history has enough evidence to show that in every recurrence of social anarchy, man's mentality reverts to the primitive mentality. This is not surprising, because all the certitudes and beliefs that give stability to social life collapse during such crises. The two great wars in our own century saw a recrudescence of widespread belief in astrology, fortune-telling and talismans. And as for the Rome of the time of Lucretius, when science was in its infancy, it was much easier for Roman society, caught in civil war and anarchy, to slip back to the superstitious mentality of primitive man. Now, the greatness of Lucretius lies in the fact that though his own unconscious mind could not help being saturated with all the premonitions of gloom, all the irrationalism and superstition suggested by his social environment, he summoned up enough courage to fight them. He was not a scientist equipped with a fund of fully verified theories who could casually dismiss all these superstitious fears. He himself was oppressed by them and he had yet to seek a way out of this dark forest. The significance of the passage lies in the fact that we see in it, below the surface, the imagination of the poet running counter, as it were, to the argument of his powerful reason, riveting upon our senses with almost intolerable force, the beliefs he is himself seeking to dispel. We see the man himself shudder with the fear which his logic is in the act of plucking up by the roots. The fear-laden approach to the problems of human destiny is not a thing of the past, of the primitive phase; it has recurred in subsequent history and it will recur again whenever social life is seriously menaced. And during every such crisis, man will have to undertake afresh that sombre struggle with the weaknesses and fears buried deep in his own unconscious, which Lucretius had to undertake in his period.

'As children tremble and fear everything in the blind dark,' he wrote, 'so we in the daylight some times are afraid of things which are no more to be feared than those which the children dread in the dark and imagine to be coming to attack them. This terror of the soul and this darkness must be dispelled, not by the rays of the sun and the shining shafts of the day, but by the sight of nature and reason.' Lucretius did not deny the existence of gods. But they existed so remote from our world and had so little to do with it that it was as good as if they did not exist at all. Like Confucius and the Buddha he felt that man should leave the gods alone as totally irrelevant to his own fundamental problems. Lucretius wrote:

'It is no piety to be often seen turning towards a stone or approaching every alter, nor to lie prostrate on the ground, stretching out your hands before the shrine of gods, nor to flood their altars with the blood of beasts, nor to make prayer after prayer. Piety rather lies in being able to view all things with an untroubled mind.'

The root of all unhappiness is ignorance. Man does not know nature. Therefore, he does not understand himself, nor the conditions and limits of his existence. The great poem of Lucretius is dedicated to the revelation of the laws of the material universe from which the laws of life and conduct, Lucretius believed, could be derived with logical harmony.

What perpetually transforms the work from a dull, philosophical treatise into a rich, poetic tissue is the fact that Lucretius did not advance by a cold, logical reasoning, but let his reason be warmed to a generous glow by the myriad reactions which nature produced on his rich sensibility. In woods and fields, in plants and animals, in mountain, river and sea, he found a delight rivalled only by his passion for philosophy. Nothing of nature's loveliness or terror was lost upon him. He was stirred by the forms and sounds, odours and savours of things. He felt the silences of secret haunts, the quiet falling of the night, the lazy waking of the day. Quietly, silently, immense forces were at work all round him, building up the universe, sustaining its evolution, reabsorbing into themselves forms of life whose function was over. It seemed to him that all the gods of mythology would be powerless to accomplish the tremendous task of sustaining the order of the universe and that only nature could do that task and nature was self-sufficient. 'For who is strong enough to rule the sum of things, to hold in hand the mighty bridle of the unfathomable sea, to turn all the planets and stars of the heavens around, to shake the serene sky with thunder, to launch the lightning that often shatters temples?' The only god is the law of nature. And the truest worship, as well as the only peace, lies in learning that law and loving it. 'The terror and gloom of the mind must be dispelled by the law of nature.'

In outlining his theory of the evolution of the universe, Lucretius accepts the atomic theory of the Greeks. Matter and space are the primary realities. Matter exists as atoms and space allows the random motion of the myriad atoms of primeval matter. They are in perpetual motion, forming groups, dissociating, regrouping. Things may look stationary, but they are caught in a heady vortex of movement.

'Often on a hill, woolly sheep go creeping wherever the dew-sparkling grass tempts them and the well-fed lambs play and butt their heads in sport. Yet in the distance all these are blurred together and seem but a whiteness resting on a green hill. Sometimes great armies cover wide fields in war manoeuvres. The brilliant bronze of their shields illumines the countryside and sends reflections into the sky. The ground trembles and thunders under their marching feet and their galloping steeds. And the mountains, buffeted by the sound, hurl it back to the very stars. But there is a place on the peaks from which these armies appear to be motionless, a little brightness resting on the plain.'

Science has confirmed this intuition of the perpetual flux of the universe. The atom which was once supposed to be a hard particle is today revealed as a solar system of particles in very rapid motion.

One major difficulty created by the older material-ism was the fact that the inertness of matter made it move only under the action of external forces and as man's body is also made up of matter, the conclu-sion became inescapable that all his motions were similarly due to external forces. Lucretius solves this difficulty by claiming the power of self-movement for matter. This spontaneity runs through all things in nature and culminates in man's free will.

Lucretius goes on to describe the evolution of the world from the hot gases that formed the primeval nebula. A tiny fragment of this nebula cooled to form the earth. Earthquakes reveal that the interior of the earth still consists of hot gases under pressure. Similarly, thunder and lightning and rain are all natural phenomena and not the anger or bounty of unseen gods in the sky.

Life evolved from the organisation of matter. Forms of animal life arose and to explain their evolution, Lucretius formulates a struggle for existence and natural selection, two thousand years before Darwin. Changes in structure appear at random and those which are useful for survival confer advantages in

selection to the forms of life possessing them. 'Nothing arises in the body in order that we may use it,
but what arises brings forth its own use ... Many
were the monsters that the earth tried to make, some
without feet, and others without hands or mouth or
face. It was in vain. Nature denied them growth, nor
could they find food, or join in the way of life. Many
kinds of animals must have perished then, for those
to which nature gave no protective qualities lay at
the mercy of others, and were soon destroyed.'

Social organisation gave man the power to survive
animals far stronger than himself. He discovered fire
from the friction of dry leaves and boughs, developed languages from gestures, and learned songs
from the birds. He tamed animals for his use, and
himself with marriage and law. He tilled the soil,
wove clothing, moulded metals into tools, observed
the heavens, measured time, learned navigation,
built cities and states. History is a procession of
states and civilisations rising, prospering, decaying,
dying. But each in turn transmits the civilising heritage of customs, morals and arts. 'Like runners in a
race, they hand on the torches of life.'

Lucretius next turns to the problems of ethics. All
misery arises from excessive ambition. 'To seek
power, which is an empty thing, and ever to labour

sore in that pursuit, is nothing but struggling to push up the mountain a stone which rolls back from the very top and bounds away to the flat lands of the plains.' Lucretius wanted men to pause once in a while and contemplate the meaning of what they were incessantly trying to do. 'Pleasant it is, when the winds make turmoil on the mighty sea, to watch the hard toil of others from the land. Not that the distress of any man gives delight, but because it is sweet to see the ills which you yourself escape. But nothing is sweeter than to dwell in the serene, well fortified sanctuaries built by the teachings of the wise, whence you may look down on others. Unhappy minds of men! Blind hearts! In what darkness of life, in what dangers, does our little time go by! Virtue lies not in the fear of the gods, nor in the timid shunning of pleasure. It lies in the harmonious operation of senses and faculties guided by reason. 'The real wealth of men is to live simply with a mind at peace.'

Empedocles, the Greek philosopher, had formulated attraction and repulsion as the two great forces behind cosmic processes. At the level of matter, these forces explain the formation of compounds from elements. In evolution they emerge as the struggle for survival and the group solidarity that helps survival. As civilisation advances, man should try to achieve his purposes more and more by cooperation than by conflict. Lucretius regards love as the great creative power behind the evolution of nature and begins his great work with a prayer to Venus, the goddess of love, conceived as a symbol of creative desire and the ways of peace.

'Through thee, every kind of life is conceived and born, and looks upon the sun. Before thee and thy coming, the winds flee and the clouds of the sky depart. To thee the miraculous earth lifts up sweet flowers. For thee the waves of the sea laugh and the peaceful heavens shine with overspreading light. As soon as the spring-time face of the day appears, and the fertilising south wind makes all things fresh and green, then first the birds of the air proclaim thee and thy advent, O divine one, pierced to the heart by thy power. Then the wild herds leap over the glad pastures and cross the swift streams. So, held captive by thy charm, each one follows thee wherever thou goest to lead. Then through seas and mountains and rushing rivers, and the leafy dwellings of the birds, thou strikest soft love into the breasts of all creatures, and makest them to propagate their generations after their kinds. Since, therefore, thou alone rulest the nature of things, since without thee nothing rises to the shining shores of light, nothing joyful or lovely is born, I long for thee as a partner in the writing of these verses. Cause, meanwhile, the savage works of war to sleep and be still. Persuade your lover, the war god, to forget all conflicts in your arms and grant Romans the gifts of peace!'

In his fight against the prevailing superstitions about the terrors of life after death, in a hell full of torments, Lucretius disdained to offer any hopes about any individual immortality. He did not believe that the soul survived the body. But this did not detract from the preciousness of life. 'Life is given to none in perpetual possession, but to all only for use.' Meanwhile, it was absurd to fear death. It does remove the possibility of enjoying the good things of life, but this is not a real loss, because after death we can neither desire nor miss these things. Death therefore is nothing to us. While we live, it does not exist for us. When it exists for us, we cease to exist. In the very nature of things, it and we cannot exist together.

'Now, now no more shall a glad home and perfect wife welcome thee, nor dashing children race to snatch thy first kisses and touch spirit with a sweet silent content. Thy friends lament over thee, from whom one disastrous day has taken all these rewards of life. But this they forget to add, that now no more does any longing for those things come over thee.' Meanwhile, even if you perish, other generations take your place.

This pattern reappears in the life of the universe. All things that grow, decay: organs, organisms, families, races, planets, stars. Only the atoms never die. The forces of creation and development are balanced by the forces of destruction in a vast rhythm of life and death. Our earth itself is dying. The land is becoming exhausted, rains and rivers erode it and carry even the mountains at last into the sea. Some day our whole stellar system will suffer a like mortality. 'No single thing abides, but all things flow. Atoms cling to atoms and thus things grow until we know and name them. But by degrees they melt and are no more the things we know. Globed from the atoms, I see the suns arise, I see the star systems lift their forms. And even the systems and their suns shall go back slowly to the eternal drift. Thou too, O earth, – thine empires, lands and seas – the smallest, with thy stars, of all the galaxies, globed from the drift like these, like these thou too shalt go. Thou art going hour by hour like these. Nothing abides. Thy seas are ever going off in delicate haze. Those crescent-shaped sandy shores shall forsake their place. The seas shall recede and then, ages afterwards, other seas shall flow back and mow with their scythes of whiteness other bays.' But throughout all this change, the vitality of the world remains invincible. 'The wailing of the new-born infant is mingled with the dirge sung over the dead.' New systems form, new stars and planets, another earth, and fresher life. Another vast cycle of evolution begins again.

Lucretius wrote one generation before Virgil and his poem is perhaps intrinsically greater than any work of Virgil's. But the poet of the recurring cycle of creation and dissolution operated on too vast a range to become the national poet. For him, there was nothing special about Rome's imperial destiny. She was one of the numerous empires of the earth, destined to flourish for a time and then disappear. His abhorrence of war did not suit the statesmen who were building up an empire. He rejected religion while traditional religion was felt by others to be a power contributing to social stability. The greatness of Lucretius necessarily transcended his country and epoch. If he could not become the poet of his nation, he has become something greater, the poet of the human race. 'Grant to my words an undying beauty,' he had prayed to Venus in his opening invocation. We can see that the prayer was granted.

After Lucretius, the philosophical tradition in poetry concentrated more on social criticism and thus the satire was born. Satire had emerged in Greek literature also, but its development in Rome was from purely national sources. In rural Italy, there was the practice of singing comic songs ridiculing village types during holidays and festivals. The Atellan comedy developed out of this tradition. Independently, it also gave rise to the satirical poem. It was Ennius who first adapted it, refined its grossness, softened its asperity and deepened it with philosophical ideas and thus elevated it to a literary form which became very popular. As Roman comedy imitated the later Greek comedy of manners and not the comedy of Aristophanes, it was not effective as a vehicle of social criticism. Therefore, the satire took over this function and became a very effective tool of social comment.

After Ennius, Lucilius (180–104 BC) is the first great satirist. His social position helped the satire to become outspoken, because he was a great-uncle of Pompey and his victims could not easily silence him, as they might have been able to do, if he was a smaller man. Lucilius has survived only in fragments. In one of his satires, a council is held in heaven to discuss the affairs of humankind at large and to consider the best method of prolonging the Roman State. Lucilius notes that luxury and avarice are ruining the upper classes while superstition is killing the initiative of the commoners. The love of gold has proved to be destructive of all honesty, good faith and every religious principle. He gives a comic picture of the miser. 'His bag and all the money he has, he carries with him. He sups with his bag, sleeps with it, bathes with it. The man's whole hope centres in his bag alone. All the rest of his existence is bound up in this bag.' In another passage, he attacks the crafty and dishonest tricks of pleaders. In yet another satire, he contrasts the frugal simplicity and tranquil leisure of rustic life with the empty vanities and arrogant manners of the ambitious townsman. In one of his satires, he attempts a new form. It is a travel diary and describes a journey which he took from Rome to Capua and from there to the Straits of Messina, with an account of some of the places on his route and incidents of travel. Criticisms of literary men and social weaknesses are offered as incidental comments. Horace later adopted this form in his description of a journey to Brundisium.

We have seen that Catullus effectively used verse to ridicule his unfaithful mistress and her other lovers. He also satirised political personalities and there is a small poem of his attacking Pompey:

> *Behold our fierce hero*
> *He scratches his head.*
> *What wants he, I wonder?*
> *A mate for his bed?*

Horace (65–8 BC) wrote literary criticism as well as lyrical poetry besides satires. His father was originally a slave who was subsequently freed and became a tax-collector. The old man saved all his money to send Horace for his education to Rome and then to Athens and Horace recalled with gratitude throughout his life, the self-sacrifices of his affectionate father. Horace was a student at Athens when Caesar was assassinated. He joined the civil war on the side of Brutus and against Octavian and its end found him ruined. He had to earn his livelihood as a clerk in Rome. Luckily Virgil developed a liking for the young man and introduced him to Maecenas, the chief minister of Augustus. Maecenas gave him a small estate in the Sabine hills and Horace could devote himself to poetry.

Like Virgil, Horace also understood the greatness of the task of reconstruction which Augustus was undertaking and his sympathies were wholly with that great statesman. When Augustus was absent from Rome for several years, conducting campaigns in Gaul, Horace wrote a poem calling on him to return, 'Come back, good chief. Give your light to your country again. When your countenance shines on the people, like spring, the days go by more gladly and the suns have a fairer light. As a mother sighs for her son, so the country, smitten by loyal yearning, wants its ruler.' The language is courtly, but the feeling was sincere, for Augustus brought peace to a country ruined by civil war. 'Thanks to you, the ox roams in safety over the meadows, kindly abundance nourishes the land, the sailors ply over a peaceful sea and honour shrinks from the very breath of blame. Your age has brought plenty to the fields, imposed right restraint on unreined licence, driven out crime and called back the old virtues by which the Latin name and the might and glory of Italy grew great, and the majesty of our empire reached from the rising of the sun to his bed in the west.'

In 17 BC, Augustus instituted the National Games, the great festival of legendary Rome, which had not been held for many centuries due to the disorder in the land. The occasion was as important as the Olympic Games of Greece and as Pindar had been chosen to compose the choral songs for those festivals in Greece, Horace was selected for the Roman festival. 'Bountiful sun, dispensing light, wherever you voyage in your shining car, may you see nothing greater than Rome! May the earth be fertile in fruits and beasts and may the healthful rain and winds of Jupiter nurture the seeds in the bosom of the earth! May the goddess of fortune grant happy marriages to our maidens and bring forth a new generation abundantly!' Unlike Catullus and others, Horace called upon the Roman youth to fight for their country and not as the knights of Venus, the goddess of love. 'Let the Roman youth, stalwart in hard warfare, learn to suffer cramping poverty as his mate. Let him resist the ferocious tribesman, formidable on his horse, with his lance in his hand.' Like Augustus, he saw the importance of bringing new life to rural Italy. He had a genuine love for the countryside and his poems give unforgettable pictures of the pageant of the seasons as they changed the face of the landscape. Here is a description of winter: 'The mountain peak stands, one dazzling mass of solid snow. The bent woods fret beneath their load of snow. And, bound by the frost, the streams have ceased to flow.' In another poem, he gives an extended description of the life of the farmer.

'He weds the tender vine-shoots, budding into life, to tall trees. He guides his wandering herds to some green valley among the hills, shears his sheep in the sunshine and stores the liquid honey in fragrant jars. When autum comes over the smiling land and the trees are crowned with rosy apples, he makes a rich harvest. At noon he rests on the grassy turf in the shade of an ancient tree, while streams glide nearby with low murmurs, the birds sing among the deep thickets and the mountain springs sing a lullaby inducing gentle sleep.'

Horace felt that the traditional religion of Rome contributed greatly to social stability. In the rural areas, religious worship was a simple ritual, entering unobtrusively into the day's rhythm of work and leisure. It merely consisted of offering flowers or the first grain and fruits of the harvest to the guardian deities whose images were set up in fields or woods. In one poem, he pays a sensitive homage to Faunus, the god of the tiller and herdsman:

'God of prosperity, fleet-foot lover of flying wood-nymphs, enter my sunlit farmland and gently look on my flocks with its many newly-dropped young. Bless and gently go. On your festival day, wine shall be poured before your image and your ancient altar shall smoke with fragrant incense. Then, when the harvest is over and the unyoked oxen rest where the streams flow, young lambs shall frisk in the flowering grasses and the villagers shall dance, while the gold and crimson leaves shed by the autumnal trees fall at thy feet in a continuous shower.'

One of his poems is entitled the *Art of Poetry* and is a letter in verse to a young friend who wanted to take up a literary career. Horace wants the writer to study life and philosophy, for without observation and understanding, even a perfect style is an empty thing. Feeling is essential but mere emotion does not make a poem. Art is not raw feeling but feeling worked into perfect form. Clarity should be the ideal and long and pedantic words should be avoided. If the writer chooses drama, the action and not the words should tell the story and delineate the characters. Horror should not be represented on the stage. The unities of time, place and action should be obeyed. The writer should try to mingle the useful with the pleasant, for the ideal book is that which entertains and instructs at the same time.

We now come to his satires. Occasionally, 'the smoke and wealth and noise of Rome and the ignorant and evil-thinking crowd' irritate him so much that he becomes very abusive. But generally, he avoided the personal abuse freely resorted to by an earlier satirist like Lucilius and dealt only with types. If Virgil's peasants are too idealised and the men and women in Ovid are too depraved to be representative, Horace introduces us to the real citizens of urban Rome. We meet the clever and impertinent slave, the vain poet, the pompous lecturer, the greedy philosopher, the talkative bore, the money-mad businessman, the ambitious statesman. The style is colloquial. The types range from the miser who buries his hoard in a hole in the ground to the stoic philosopher to whom life is so remote that 'all the vices are equal.' He traces all aberrant social types to the lack of moderation. The gourmets feed inordinately on delicacies and suffer acutely due to indigestion. He laughs at the money-crazy business-man who amasses wealth but cannot enjoy it. For the hunter of legacies, he gives tips on how to murder their prospective benefactors. Going for a morning walk, he is pounced upon by a social climber who wants an introduction to Maecenas. He is amused at the restless people who, while in the city, long for the country and when they get there, start longing to return to the city; who can never enjoy what they have because there is some one who has more; who grumble about the evils of the times but will refuse to go back to the old days if some god were to offer to take them.

Horace, was not a stern hater of pleasures. He was more a follower of Epicurus and believed in the legitimacy of reasonable pleasures. He knew how brief was our allotted span, how inexorable was the steady march of time. 'Our years glide silently away. No tears, no amount of prayers, repair the wrinkled cheek, the whitening hair that drop forgotten to the tomb ... White-faced death comes alike to the pauper's shack and the palaces of kings. The little sum of life forbids the ravelling of lengthy hopes. Night and the world of the dead are near. We are nearing the empty house, past whose threshold, you will meet no wine like this.' Why plan so carefully a future whose shape will laugh at our plans? Youth and beauty touch us and flee away. Let us enjoy them now. Even as we speak, envious time runs out. Let us seize the occasion, snatch the day, before sunset arrives. Youth is the time for happiness and the happiness is legitimate. 'The pleasing whisper in the dark, the half-unwilling, willing kiss, the laugh that guides you to the mark, when the kind maid feigns coyness, but hides only to be found again—these are joys which the gods have ordained for youth.' But there should be a moderation in every thing, if pleasure is not to bring disgust in its wake. The simple life is the best. He preferred his own country estate to Rome, 'My stream of pure water, my few acres of woodland, my sure trust in a crop of corn, bring me more blessing than the lot of the man who has vast estates in fertile Africa.' To the question who is free, he gave this answer: 'The wise man, who is lord over himself, whom neither poverty nor death affright, who defies his passions, scorns ambition, and is in himself a whole. If a man is just and resolute, the whole world may break and fall upon him and find him, in the ruins, undismayed.' When death approached, it found him prepared to quit life contentedly 'like a guest who had his fill.' He told himself: 'You have played enough, eaten enough, drunk enough; it is now time for you to go.' He died within a few months of the death of his friend and patron Maecenas and was laid to rest near his tomb.

The satire in the Roman tradition was a fairly flexible form. It did not always employ ridicule as a weapon. Moral literature which called upon people to change their undesirable social traits was also included in satires. The writings of Persius (AD 34–62) illustrate this development. This young man had an ardent mind, devoted to literature and intellectual pleasures, of a philosophical turn and a chastened though somewhat fastidious taste. We can see that he laments the corruption of public taste as much as he deplores the decay of public morals. There is the warmth of feeling and eloquence throughout, but sarcasm itself is employed only occasionally.

The young idealist emphasises that freedom consists in virtue alone and that none but the philosopher can be truly virtuous and free in this sense. Even if only one vice remains and all the other passions have been mastered, man will continue to remain enslaved, whether it be avarice, luxury, superstition or ambition. He warns those who are ambitious of becoming leaders, that they should first seriously consider whether they have the necessary qualifications, experience, education and talent, for the task. Once embarked on their career, they must be continuously alert in self-examination. Persius keenly felt the tragedy of Roman youth steadily going down the path of degradation and attacked their pride, love of luxury and aversion to work.

'You are moist, soft earth. You ought to be taken instantly and fashioned by the rapid wheel. But you do not like this. You have a paternal estate with a fine crop of corn and bright vessels for your banquets. Are you going to be satisfied with it? Do you think it is decent to puff yourself up because you are thousandth in the line from some ancient Tuscan family? Off with your swanky dress! I can look under them and see your skin. Are you not ashamed to live the loose life of a rake? The rake's condition is well-known to you. He is paralysed by vice. His heart is overgrown by thick layers of fat. He feels no reproach. He knows nothing of his loss. He is sunk in the depth and makes no more bubbles on the surface. But you hear the voice that whispers to your heart, "we are going, going down a precipice".'

When he found that the young men lived in idleness, in expectation of legacies from rich relatives, he called upon the latter not to stint themselves to leave their wealth to profligates who would squander them in no time. In one of his satires, a rich man takes the advice and says: 'Am I to live on cheap food even on festival days, so that a spendthrift grandson may one day stuff himself with rich food and, when the fancy takes him, lavish money on a mistress? Am I to live a thread-bare skeleton, so that his fat paunch may sway from side to side?' Persius also advised people to use wealth and not abuse it. Wealth, according to him, had a social responsibility and he pleaded for prompt and liberal regard to the necessities and distresses of others.

Persius realised that, though man had multipled his wants unnecessarily, the effort he had to put in justified somewhat the luxury he enjoyed. 'Our flesh, our sensuous appetites, spoil wholesome oil by mixing fragrant essences with it; steep wool in all sorts of colours that were made for no such use; tear the pearl from the oyster; and separate the veins of glowing gold ore from the primitive slag. It sins. Yes, it sins. But it wins by effort what it gets.' But he could not understand the sense in lavishing such hard-earned wealth in religious worhsip. It brought no returns and it made religion unnecessarily ornate. 'You reverend priests, tell me what good gold can do in a holy place.' He then goes on to analyse the psychology of popular religion and worhsip. The habit of making costly offerings springs from the mental confusion of people who regard God as depraved as the men in power in their own society and seek to propitiate him with the bribes which the latter demand for granting favours. A business contract is thus sought to be established between themselves and heaven. He concludes with a noble interpretation of what constitutes real prayer.

'Justice to god and man enshrined within the heart; the inner chambers of the soul free from pollution; the heart imbued with a sense of honour. Let me have these to carry to the temple.'

Scattered in the satires of Persius are sound comments of literary criticism. He deplores that oratory has decayed. The manly eloquence of Cato and the dignity of Virgil have been diluted by the introduction of redundant and misplaced metaphor, trifling conceits, accumulated epithets, bombastic and obsolete words and a substitution of rhetorical tricks for that energetic simplicity which speaks from the heart to the heart. He ridiculed the versifier without inspiration who begged his livelihood from the rich who pretended to have literary tastes. 'Listen. The rich men of Rome are sitting after a full meal and enquiring while drinking, "what news from the divine world of poesy?" Thereupon a person in a queer dress brings out some mawkish trash or other, with a snuffle and a lisp, something about some Phyllis or any of the many heroines over whom poets have snivelled, filtering out his tones and tipping up the words against the roof of his delicate mouth.' Only genuine and intense feeling can help poetry recover its lost greatness. 'A man's tears must come from his heart, at the moment, not from his brains overnight, if he is to move me with his tragic narration.'

In Sulpicia, who lived towards the end of the first century AD, the satire becomes almost wholly a piece of moral and political literature. Emperor Domitian, who found that thinkers were the greatest enemies of autocracy, passed an edict expelling them from Rome and it was this development which provoked Sulpicia to write her satire. She warns that the effect of such an edict would be nothing less than forcing the civilised world to revert to a state of primeval barbarism. Curiously enough, she traces the cause of such a reactionary development to a long protracted peace. Perhaps she meant that the order established by an autocratic regime was really like the peace of the grave. When Rome was struggling against Greece, her hardy and martial temper was maintained, the citizens were united in a sentiment of patriotism and the leaders were tolerant enough to appreciate the value of Greek learning. The satire concludes with a prophecy of coming vengeance against the tyrant.

If the satire becomes eloquent political literature in the case of Sulpicia, it moves to the opposite end of its range in Martial (AD 40–102) who throughout used ridicule for his attack and very often became even obscene. He was born in Spain but came to Rome to seek his fortune. He did not fare well. He had to live in a garret, humiliate himself with the rich for his daily meals, work for a publisher who cheated him. Towards the end of his life, he got disgusted with Rome. The younger Pliny gave him the money to go back to Spain, where he acquired a rich mistress and lived in comparative comfort till his death.

In the history of satire, the importance of Martial lies in the fact that he perfected epigrammatic verse for vigorous attack. Originally, the epigram was not an exclusively satirical form. The epitaphs in the Greek anthology are epigrams but their mood is tragic and tender. But Greek poets like Demodocus had used it for satire. Martial moulded it into a brief, sharp form, barbed with a satiric sting. There is a twist of thought in his epigrams, the reader being led casually to the end of the verse when the point of the satire suddenly explodes in the last line, taking him by surprise. Both Martial and Statius sought the patronage of Emperor Domitian. Statius was lucky here and the frustrated Martial declared that a live epigram was worth more than a dead epic, the reference being to the epic on the Theban story written by Statius. In his claim, Martial was not far wrong, for the heavy manner of the epic was becoming unpopular and Martial's epigrammatic style became very popular with the cynical Roman society.

Martial often wrote very obscene verses. He was shrewd enough to claim that those who decried his

obscenity in public relished it in private. 'The young
lady blushed and laid down my volume, but that was
because she had company. Let them go away and she
will read it.' But it looks as if he himself became, on
occasion, ashamed of his obscenity and he hastened
to assure the reader that though his lines were
licentious, his life was chaste. He also claimed that
his method of attack was very different from that of
the earlier writers, who abused persons by name.
Martial himself attacked types and this is what gives
its importance to his poetry. The corrupt society, in
which his own lot was cast, is brilliantly resurrected
for us. We meet men from all strata of society, from
the barber to the literary critic. About a barber, he
says that he works so slow that while he shaves, the
beard grows again. He laughs at a critic who affects
contempt for contemporary writers and is willing to
praise only the writers of the past, and adds: 'I, alas,
live and do not consider it worth my while to die so
that I can win a word of praise from him.'

Being poor, he probably had little success in his love
affairs and he was merciless to the society women of
Rome. 'She swears that the golden hair that lends
her beauty is hers. I know she swears true, for I know
where she bought it.' In another poem, he goes into
details. 'Your tresses are manufactured far away.
You lay aside your teeth at night just as you do your

silk dresses. Your beauty lies stored away in a hundred caskets and your face does not sleep with you. You wink with an eyelash brought to you in the morning. No respect moves you for your outworn carcass, which you may now count as one of your ancestor's.' In another poem, he goes to the extreme. He enumerates all the evil smells of the slums of Rome and adds: 'All these stenches I prefer to yours, lady.'

Legacy hunting had become the universal occupation of Rome's high society. Martial laughs at a man who puts on mourning for his dead wife, because he knows that he wooed and won his bride in her seventieth year, 'all for love, together with property worth two million.' When a host serves him wine, the poet refers to the rumour that poisoned wine had accounted for four of his host's wives, loudly protests that he knows the rumour is all a lie, but pleads that just then he does not feel the need for a drink. To a rich man who is unwilling to help the poet with a loan but who says that he will leave the poet a substantial sum in his legacy, Martial says: 'You must be mad beyond redress, if my next wish you cannot guess!' Martial notes that the richer men become, the more close-fisted they turn. He reminds an acquaintance that he was very liberal when he had only a bare hundred thousand. Four legacies in quick succession brought him a million. The poet reminds him that it was his prayer that did the trick, since the legacies all came from men who were healthy and were not expected to die for a long time. But since getting so rich, the man has become very miserly. He gives only one feast a year and even that looks as if all he spent was one counterfeit coin. The poet concludes by saying that he will fervently pray that his friend gets another ten million. For, at this rate, with ten million, the rich man will not only not give anything to his friends, but starve himself to death.

Martial is not always on the attack. There are quieter moments which reveal certain unsuspected, likable traits in him. He could relax and enjoy life, if the mood was right. In one short poem, he complains that men fritter away their energy in stupid ambitions without pausing to enjoy life. 'Dead to our better selves, we see the golden hours take flight, scoring dead losses to us as they flee. Let us therefore hasten to live right.' In another poem, he defines the ingredients of a happy life. 'Some acres of a kindly soil, health, a peaceful mind, plain living, no law suits, friends, evenings of temperate gaiety, the pot unfailing on the fire, a discreet but bright wife, sound slumber that lends wings to night. If you have these, you do not have to long for death nor fear it when it comes.' He has given a pleasant description

of his own small house. It was on a hill and com-
manded a fine view of Rome. The air was very pure
on these heights and it retained a radiant sunshine
even when the surrounding hills and valleys were
enveloped in mists. The clear stars seemed so near
as to look like decorations on the roof. 'Here the
sea's bosom gently quivers in the breeze. The wind
is gentle as if some maiden were fanning herself in
the boats. The fisherman need not go to the deep
sea, but casts his line near the shore and in the clear
water he can even see the fish coming to take his
bait.' He had a sure taste in sculpture and painting
and in one couplet he praises the marvellous realism
of the work of Phidias, the Greek sculptor. 'Phidias
wrought these fishes. They have been endowed with
life by him. Add water and they will swim.'

It is with pleasant surprise that we note that Martial's verse could communicate sorrow with an
exceptional purity of accent. When the little daughter of a friend of his died, he wrote this epitaph:

> *Soft were her tiny bones, then soft be the sod that*
> *enshrouds her!*
> *Gentle be thy touch, mother earth, gently she*
> *rested on thee.*

When a young slave to whom he was attached died,
he mourned him like a brother. 'Dear youth, too

early lost, who now art laid beneath the turf in this green mountain valley! I will raise over you no tombstone or carved sculpture, to crumble, as time goes by, with your crumbling dust. But the creeper of the vine shall wave the shadows of its leaves over your resting place and the grass, bedewed with tears, shall clothe thy grave. My sorrowing heart shall bring to thee these gifts, which will ever be fresh and deathless as the spring. And when my hour comes, let my tomb also be as lowly and as green!'

About Juvenal (AD 60–140), the last great Roman satirist, we do not have many biographical details. He was born in a village southeast of Rome and seems to have practised law in the capital. According to tradition, he wrote and circulated among his friends a satire on Domitian, for which he was expelled to Egypt for a few years. In any case, Juvenal published nothing till after Domitian's death.

In the opening section of his *Satires*, he attacks the versifiers who go unpunished though murderously prolific and declares himself determined to produce as much waste paper as the rest. In such an age when virtue is praised but vice practised, the age of the libertine, the social climber, the forger and the murderer, it is hard not to write satire. 'All the daily life of Rome shall be my theme,' he says.

The weakness of Juvenal lies in his strong prejudices. His two pet aversions were foreigners and women. He condemned the Jew as clannish. He is especially bitter against the Greek. Grown crafty and greedy in decadence, the Greek has made himself the master of the Roman, by his flattery and cunning. But the greatest enemy of man, in his opinion, is woman. He accuses the women of Rome of every vice and crime. A good woman is stranger than a white crow. He is appalled to see that one of his friends is contemplating marriage. He thinks that even suicide is a better alternative and asks his friend why he wants to marry when it is so easy to jump off a bridge or a high window or find a rope to hang himself. He hated most the learned woman who could quote Virgil at you. 'O, may the gods save us from a learned wife!'

Nevertheless, in many of his attacks, he was able to seize real tendencies of social decay. He spared no class, from the highest to the lowest. The autocratic emperors roused his greatest wrath. Nero had loved to play the role of Orestes in Greek dramas. Juvenal was willing to forgive the fact that, like Orestes, Nero had murdered his own mother. But he was not willing to forgive the emperor for writing a tiresome epic on Troy and for singing on the public stage. Coming to Domitian, he draws a comic picture of his whole cabinet seriously discussing the question of what to do with an unusually large fish that somebody had caught and presented to the emperor. Juvenal draws inimitable pictures of Domitians' servile councillors. One of them turns to his right and goes into an ecstatic description of the fish, while it is really to his left on the table; his eyesight is very poor. Another tells the emperor that this is an augury that he will have a big triumph and take some mighty king as captive. At last the cabinet decides to cook the fish whole. The poet asks in conclusion: 'Ah, why did not Domitian devote himself entirely to such trifles as these?' He attacks the aristocracy for its many degenerate habits and is especially indignant against the members of that class who became governors, looted the provinces and settled down to a life of extravagant luxury. He does not spare the commoners either. Once they controlled the armies and could make and unmake kings, but now they could be bought with 'bread and circuses'; that is, subsidised corn and spectacular amusements made them forget to fight for their political rights. Juvenal seems to have been alive to the growing danger from the army. The soldier could get summary settlement of all his disputes, while the unhappy civilian, assaulted by a soldier, could not get redress, for such cases were heard in camps by army officers. The city had become congested and unhealthy. The streets are so crowded that the pedestrian does not walk, but is carried along in the press. Waggons lumber by, filled with huge timber, stretching on either side and leading to numerous accidents. It is worse during the nights. Broken crockery flung out of the windows hits the predestrian and if he escapes it, he is victimised by thieves and highway robbers.

The sombre pessimism of Tacitus seems to have affected Juvenal also. At times he seems to be without any hope of redemption for his country. 'We are arrived at the zenith of vice and posterity will never be able to surpass us.' But, at bottom, he fervently prayed for a social regeneration and was confident that it could be achieved. His view about the evolution of civilisation is as far reaching as that of Lucretius. Plant and animal forms have vitality only. Man has a soul in addition and by soul Juvenal means nothing more mysterious than emotional sensitiveness, an instinct of affection which moves us spontaneously when we see the distress of others. It was this reciprocally shared instinct of affection which helped primitive groups to evolve into civilised societies. This sentiment of unity helped men to emerge from the ancient wood and abandon the forests where our primitive ancestors had lived, to build houses in settlements so that the confidence mutually engendered by a neighbour's threshold might add security to our slumbers, to extend our helping hand to our fallen comrades. But today this sense of belonging to one family has been lost. While animal species attack only other species and do not wage intergroup wars, people have stopped making ploughshares in their forges and are now busy making swords to kill each other. Juvenal blames avarice and the self-centred existence for this utter debasement of man and this leads him to the problems of ethics.

In addition to an exaggerated anxiety about security, it is the desire to be held as different from others, to be regarded as superior to them, that makes men seek power, as a source of distinction, with inordinate avarice. First of all Juvenal satirises those people who think that distinction can be inherited, by descent in great families or from ancestors with achievements to their credit. Distinction, on the other hand, is personal and must be won by one's own achievements. Now even here, we must be careful not to waste our life and energy in seeking worthless goals. Wealth, power and military glory have too often proved inconstant and in the end, worthless as objectives of human effort. With immense effort Hannibal led an army across the Alps. But ultimately he was completely defeated and had to commit suicide. His only achievement, in retrospect, seems to have been providing material for a lesson in the schoolchild's history textbook.

Time, always in rapid flight, withers all blooms, and even as youth is stretching its hand towards a glass of wine or a slender waist, old age is drawing near. The only solution is to learn to enjoy the present with content, rejecting transient pleasures with the help of the disciplined moral sense and awaiting the future with calmness. Juvenal advocates the simple life and high thinking. It is better to get out of the lunatic asylum called Rome and live in some quiet rural town where one can meet honest men and be free from the company of the stupid and the crooked. 'Put ambition behind you. The goal is not worth the striving. So long and costly is effort and so brief is fame. Cultivate your garden, desire only so much as hunger and thirst, cold and heat, demand. Seek health and contentment of mind. Guiltless of hate and proof against vain desires, bear the load of life with manliness and learn to bear pain. And do not pray for an unduly long life. Count it rather a privilege given to you by nature to die when your appointed hour comes.'

But, this should not mean that existence should become self-centred. Juvenal always emphasised that society could progress only if every individual had a sense of belonging to the family of man. Human wants depend upon mutual aid for their satisfaction and mutual love should be the inspiration behind this cooperative and reciprocal effort. 'Only a feeling of

kinship can improve our state.' Instead of preaching
a generous, but vague idealism, Juvenal specifically
directs the attention of his contemporaries to the
areas of social life neglected by society. He points
out that the high cost of living engendered by the
luxury and extravagance of the rich makes it more
and more difficult for the poor to subsist, that they
are condemned to live in slums in the dangerously
congested city, that the want of a well regulated
police subjects them to numberless miseries, that
they are universally exposed to scorn and insult, that
the loss from all this will have to be met by the whole
society, since the potential leadership in the lower
income groups does not get the opportunity to grow
and contribute to the general progress. While Quintilian wrote on the theory of education, Juvenal
concentrated on the economic disabilities of the
teachers. This class, which was vested with the great
responsibility of moulding the character of the next
generation, was expected to be omniscient, but had
to lead lives of complete drudgery on starvation
wages. He recalls the past, especially in Greece,
when teachers had enjoyed a much better status and
pays a touching homage to the honoured tutors of the
past, now a slighted race:

> *Shades of our sires! O, sacred be your rest*
> *And lightly lie the turf upon your breast!*

*Flowers on your urns breathe sweets beyond
    compare
And spring eternal shed its influence there!*

Juvenal loved children and as the future destiny of
the state depended on them, he pleaded that the
greatest care should be taken about their training.
More for their children than for themselves, he
wanted parents to maintain a healthy and fine
domestic environment and give the growing generation ideal models for conduct. And finally, he
reminded the empire builders of Rome that conquest of territory alone was not sufficient and that
without self-conquest and restraint, the conquered
realms were likely to be more free in the real sense
than the conquering state itself. 'Though Britain
trembles at our sway and islands that slumber in the
frozen polar seas and the blue ocean receive our
chain, how can we boast of conquest? O, Rome, the
conquered climes are free from your detested crimes.'

We conclude our account of Roman thought and
poetry here. The Roman achievement equals and
sometimes surpasses the tradition of Greece, especially in poetry. The influence of the great prior
tradition of Greece is, however, evident. Lucretius
helps us to see the destiny of the human race against
the background of the vast panorama of evolving

and decaying worlds, while Virgil shows us that each individual and social group, in spite of its brief span, can make its life significant by ordering it in the light of enduring moral principles.

Bibliography

Abbott, P. *The Comon People of Ancient Rome*, New York, 1911.

Apuleius, *The Golden Ass*, Tr. W. Adlington, New York, 1927.

Arnold, W. *Roman System of Provincial Administration*, Oxford, 1914.

Bailey, C. *The Legacy of Rome*, Oxford, n.d.

Bieber, M. *History of the Greek and Roman Theater*, Princeton, 1939.

Boissier, G. *Cicero and His Friends*, New York, n.d.

Boissier, G. *La Religion Romaine*, Paris, 1909.

Boissier, G. *Tacitus and Other Roman Studies*, London, 1906.

Bouchier, E. *Life and Letters in Roman Africa*, Oxford, 1913.

Britain, A. *Roman Women*, Philadelphia, 1907.

Buchan, J. *Augustus*, New York, 1937.

Buckland, W. *Textbook of Roman Law*, Cambridge University Press, 1921.

Bury, J. *History of the Roman Empire*, New York, n.d.

Caesar, J. *De Bello Civili*, Loeb Library.

Caesar, J. *De Bello Gallico*, Loeb Library.

Cato, M. *De Agricultura*, Loeb Library.

Catullus, *Poems*, Tr. Horace Gregory, New York, 1931.

Catullus, Tibullus, and Pervigilium Veneris, Loeb Library.

Charlesworth, M. *Trade Routes and Commerce of the Roman Empire*, Cambridge University Press, 1926.

Cicero, *Academica*, Loeb Library.

Collingwood, R. and Myres, N. *Roman Britian*, Oxford, 1937.

Columella, *De Re Rustica*, Loeb Library.

Cumount, F. *Oriental Religions in Roman Paganism*, Chicago, 1911.

Davis, W. *Influence of Wealth in Imperial Rome*, New York, 1913.

Declareuil, J. *Rome the Law-Giver*, New York, 1926.

Dennis, G. *Cities and Cemeteries of Etruria*, Everyman Library.

Sir Dill, S. *Roman Society from Nero to Marcus Aurelius*, London, 1911.

Duff, J. *Literary History of Rome*, London, 1909.

Duff, J. *Literary History of Rome in the Silver Age*, New York, 1930.

Fowler, W.W. *Religious Experience of the Roman People*, London, 1933.

Fowler, W.W. *Social Life at Rome*, New York, 1927.

Frank, T.   *Economic History of Rome*, Baltimore, 1927.

Frank, T.   *Roman Imperialism*, New York, 1914.

Frank, T.   *Economic Survey of Ancient Rome*, Baltimore, 1933.

Friedlander, L.   *Roman Life and Manners under the Roman Empire*, London, 1928.

Gibbon, E.   *Decline and Fall of the Roman Empire*, Everyman Library.

Guhl, E. and Koner, W.   *Life of the Greeks and the Romans*, New York, 1876.

Gummere, R.   *Seneca the Philosopher*, Boston, 1922.

Hadzsits, G.   *Lucretius and his Influence*, London, 1935.

Haskell, H.   *The New Deal in Old Rome*, New York, 1939.

Heitland, W.   *Agricola*, Cambridge University Press, 1921.

Henderson, B.   *Life and Principate of the Emperor Hadrian*, New York, n.d.

Henderson, B.   *Life and Principate of the Emperor Nero*, Philadelphia, 1903.

Herodian,   *History of Twenty Caesars*, London, 1629.

Holmes, T.R.   *The Architect of the Roman Empire*, Oxford, 1928.

Homo, L.   *Roman Political Institutions*, New York, 1930.

Horace,   *Odes and Epodes*, Loeb Library.

Horace,   *Satires and Epistles*, Loeb Library.

Jones, H. *Companion to Roman History*, Oxford, 1912.

Juvenal and Persius, *Satires*, Loeb Library.

Juvenal, Persius, Sulpicia and Lucilius, *Satires*, Tr. Gifford, London, 1852.

Livy, T. *History of Rome*, Everyman Library.

Longinus, *On the Sublime*, Loeb Library.

Lucian, *Works*, Tr. Fowler, Oxford, 1905.

Lucretius, *De Rerum Natura*, Loeb Library.

Marcus Aurelius, *Meditations*, Tr. Long, Boston, 1876.

Martial, *Epigrams*, Loeb Library.

Merivale, C. *History of the Romans under the Empire*, London, 1865.

Middleton, C. *Life of Marcus Tullius Cicero*, London, 1877.

Mommsen, T. *History of Rome*, London, 1901.

Mommsen, T. *The Provinces of the Roman Empire*, New York, 1887.

Monroe, P. *Source Book of the History of Education for the Greek and Roman Period*, New York, 1932.

Ovid, *Ars Amatoria*, Loeb Library.

Ovid, *Fasti*, Loeb Library.

Ovid, *Heroides and Amores*, Loeb Library.

Ovid, *Love Books*, Tr. May, New York, 1930.

Ovid, *Metamorphoses*, Loeb Library.

Ovid, *Tristia and Ex Ponto*, Loeb Library.

Paul-Louis, *Ancient Rome at Work*, New York, n.d.

Petronius, *Cena Trimalchionis*, Tr. W. Lowe, Cambridge, 1904.

Petronius, *Works*, Tr. M. Heseltine, Loeb Library.

Plautus, *Comedies*, London, 1889.

Pliny the Elder, *Natural History*, London, 1855.

Pliny the Younger, *Letters*, Loeb Library.

Propertius, *Poems*, Loeb Library.

Quintilian, *Institutes of Oratory*, Loeb Library.

Randall-MacIver, D. *The Etruscans*, Oxford, 1927.

Sallust, *Works*, Loeb Library.

Sir Sandys, J. *Companion to Latin Studies*, Cambridge University Press, 1925.

Scott, S.P. *The Civil Law of Rome*, Cincinnati, 1932.

Seneca, *Moral Essays*, Loeb Library.

Seneca, *Tragedies*, Loeb Library.

Smith, R.B. *Carthage and the Carthaginians*, New York, 1908.

Sellar, W. *Horace and the Elegiac Poets*, Oxford, 1937.

Sellar, W. *Roman Poets of the Augustan Age: Virgil*, Oxford, 1877.

Sellar, W. *Roman Poets of the Republic*, Oxford, 1881.

Statius, *Poems*, Loeb Library.

Strong, E. *Art in Ancient Rome*, New York, 1928.

Suetonius, *Works*, Loeb Library.

Syme, R.   *The Roman Revolution*, Oxford, 1939.

Tacitus,   *Annals*, Loeb Library.

Tacitus,   *Histories*, Loeb Library.

Tacitus,   *Works*, Tr. Murphy, London, 1830.

Taylor, H.   *Cicero*, Chicago, 1916.

Terence,   *Comedies*, London, 1898.

Varro, M.   *Rerum Rusticarum*, Loeb Library.

Virgil,   *Poems*, Loeb Library.

Vogelstein, H.   *Rome*, Philadelphia, 1940.

Watson, P.B.   *Marcus Aurelius Antoninus*, New York, 1884.

Weise, O.   *Language and Character of the Roman People*, London, 1909.

White, E.L.   *Why Rome Fell*, New York, 1927.

Wickhoff, F.   *Roman Art*, London, 1900.

Cameos in History and Culture

Orient Longman's new series brings to you short, focused, carefully written books on significant persons, places, events and processes, both past and present, from India and other parts of the world.

Each *Cameo* is on a topic of perennial interest within the broad fields of history, archaeology, anthropology and culture. The language is simple, free of jargon, yet lucid and precise. Concepts are dealt with such that they are accessible to every one.

Cameos invite you to learn more about subjects of interest to you in a manner that is exciting. These are well researched books, written by specialists.

Cameos from **Orient Longman** are available at all leading bookshops.

ALSO IN THE SERIES

Looking for the Aryans
R S Sharma

Ancient Mesopotamian Literature
Krishna Chaitanya

Ancient Egyptian Literature
Krishna Chaitanya

FORTHCOMING TITLES

Ancient Greek Literature
Krishna Chaitanya

Ancient Jewish Literature
Krishna Chaitanya